BWB Texts

Short books on big subjects from great New Zealand writers

Out of the Vaipe, the Deadwater

A Writer's Early Life

ALBERT WENDT

Published in 2015 by Bridget Williams Books Limited, PO Box 12474, Wellington 6144, New Zealand, www.bwb.co.nz, info@bwb.co.nz.

© Albert Wendt 2015

This BWB Text is copyright. Apart from fair dealing for the purpose of private study, research, criticism or review, permitted under the Copyright Act, no part may be reproduced by any process without the prior permission of the copyright holders and the publisher.

ISBN 9780908321223 (Paperback), ISBN 9780908321261 (EPUB)
ISBN 9780908321278 (KINDLE), ISBN 9780908321285 (PDF)
ISTC A0220150000000D5
DOI 10.7810/9780908321223

A catalogue record for this book is available from the National Library of New Zealand. Kei te pātenga raraunga o Te Puna Mātauranga o Aotearoa te whakarārangi o tēnei pukapuka

Acknowledgements
The publisher acknowledges the ongoing support provided by the Bridget Williams Books Publishing Trust and Creative New Zealand.

Publisher: Tom Rennie
Cover and internal design: Base Two
Editor: Geoff Walker
Typesetter: Tina Delceg
Printer: Printlink, Wellington

CONTENTS

Introduction: In Ponsonby 7

1. An Unreliable Story? 17
2. What are my Tupuaga? 38
3. Le Vaipe, the Deadwater 49
4. Is it Real? 64
5. Into a World of Books 78
6. Becoming a New Zealand Protected Person 89
7. My Mother 117
8. The Writing 128

Epilogue: The End, the Beginning 137

Editorial Note 141
About the Author 142
About BWB Texts 143

All is real, whether borrowed or created or dreamed, or mixed together with facts, fictions, strange sauces and herbs and condiments in quantities peculiar to each mixer, dreamer, cook, creator. We are all the possibilities of every creator.

All is Ola.

All is Life.

Ola (1991)

INTRODUCTION: IN PONSONBY

The yellow blooms of our leafless kōwhai tree, that leans up against the railing of our back deck, are afire with sun. Yesterday, at mid-morning, Reina, who was sitting at the table on our deck, beckoned me out and pointed up at the kōwhai. A bold young tūī, all its rich colours shimmering in the bright sunshine, was moving from bell-shaped bloom to bell-shaped bloom, in quick movements, sucking out the sweet nectar. It knew we were there but it didn't care; it was wholly in the moment, getting drunk with the nectar.

Last spring a pair of tūī built a nest at the top of the tall pōhutukawa tree at the corner of our back yard. It was the first time it had happened in our section. We believed ourselves blessed by their magnificent presence. I didn't know how ferociously territorial they were until I watched them attacking any bird that dared approach or fly by or perch in their tree. It wasn't enough scaring the intruders out of or away from their tree; they zipped and streaked after them and sometimes pecked them out of the air until they disappeared from view. Such vicious beauty.

It is October 2014, and on the 27th I'll be seventy-five. The Vaipe, the Deadwater, is where I was born and raised, in the town of Apia, Samoa. Ponsonby, Auckland, New Zealand, is where I've been living since 1992, in this villa built in 1907.

In 1991 when we saw the advertisement for the villa we arranged for the real estate agent to show us through. The first thing he told us was that Michael Joseph Savage, the first Labour Prime Minister of New Zealand, had lived there from 1908 to 1916. I was impressed by that selling point because I've always admired Mick Savage, but I wasn't going to buy an expensive house just because of it.

Reina and I really liked the villa. Then some of our friends informed us that it had been the home of Bryan Williams, the famous Samoan ex-All Black winger. Now that helped seal the deal for me.

After we had signed the deed of sale, I told the real estate agent about Bryan Williams. He chuckled and said that if he'd known that, the price would have been higher! Later Bryan heard I'd bought his family home, and wanted to come and look at how it had been renovated.

When we hosted him and his wife Leslie for lunch, he told us some of his family's history in the house where he'd spent the first seventeen years of his life. Uncanny how our histories run into each other; I found out Bryan's grandfather had been the plumber who'd hired my father as an apprentice in Samoa. Bryan's father, who must have known my father, had migrated to New Zealand when he was about seventeen. My father was only fourteen when Bryan's grandfather hired him. My father's father died in his thirties, and my father had to leave school and support his mother and a large family.

A couple of months ago, on 11 August, I had a full right-knee replacement operation at Mercy Hospital, Auckland, five years after I had had the left knee replaced. The two vertical scars look like fully grown centipedes. I'm now a double-kneed bionic still trying to recover from the latest operation, from all the types of pain that come with it.

I keep believing that seventy-five years have taught me much about physical pain and how to deal with it, but every time I experience pain anew I find myself relearning how to. And if there is a prolonged ebb-and-flow period of pain, like this one, I despair that the flow will ever end. At my age it takes longer for the body to recover from any damage – and a full knee replacement is major damage, a large invasive complicated cutting into and removal of the knee, then replacing that with a titanium joint. Before both operations, I asked the surgeons the dreaded question: what is the rate of failure and rejection? Around 1 or 2 per cent was their answer. And because the percentage was so small, I readily believed both times I wasn't going to be that percentage. This time my recovery is taking far longer than the last time. Why? Because I am five years older, I keep telling myself.

Then at night, unable to sleep because of the sporadic pain in my new knee and up and down the muscles and tendons of my leg, that easy answer is replaced with the frightening belief that I am going to suffer a major embolism and heart attack or stroke – or worse still a knee rejection, which would mean the amputation of my leg. My imagination, after years of training to conjure up all sorts of dire and fabulous scenarios for novels, is now very difficult to steer away from the darkest consequences. And being a pessimist doesn't help either. For me, turning seventy-five isn't conducive to optimism, joy and celebration.

When Reina and I returned from Hawai'i in late 2008 after spending four years teaching at the University of Hawai'i, we retired from academic life. And because our time in Hawai'i had included some of the happiest and most productive years of my life, I believed I had a long future in which to continue writing and painting, and being with Reina and my children and mokopuna. The permanent silence, the final loss of consciousness, which throughout my life has scared me to the core at times and which permeates much of my work, *felt* far away – my future would be so filled with self-renewing work that the permanent silence would be kept at bay.

I was finishing three books – a new novel; *Ancestry*, a collection of short stories; and *From Mānoa to a Ponsonby Garden*, a collection of poems – and preparing the last two for publication. We were also preoccupied with resettling into Aotearoa and Ponsonby, and being part of our large extended aiga, our family, again. The two books were published in 2012: a worthwhile achievement, I felt, containing some of my best writing.

But the new novel, which I had started writing when we arrived in Hawai'i in mid-2004, was refusing, despite many major revisions, to be captured and given the mana and power and direction I believed I could give it. Even its title remains elusive.

Previously whenever I'd been frustrated by a writing project, I'd continued with other writing, and when I'd returned to the main project I was usually able to finish it with some sense of achievement. So in this instance, I turned to painting to try and escape my despair and frustration. It didn't work. My urge to persist with the new novel defeated the diversion to paint.

Ever since I was in my twenties and getting up at about 3 a.m. and writing or studying until 5 or 6 and then sleeping again, I've nearly always woken at that time even if I don't want to. It has become habitual.

I've lived in Aotearoa since I was thirteen, but I still dread the winter cold. After four years in Hawai'i we returned home to Aotearoa with the healing sun lodged in our marrow, but the winter cold slid into our bones and sucked it out.

So feeling defeated by the new novel and unable to paint and the winter cold stinging my face and ears and heart when I woke at 3 a.m., my fertile, devious imagination and mind returned to contemplating the permanent silence – to confronting the fact that my life is finite, that seventy-five is not far from death and I certainly don't want my consciousness to end.

Over recent years many of our friends and relatives have died; the number is increasing. Death is coming closer to me. And in my dark dreams of fierce presences trying to break into my sight to smother me, I'd wake shouting, with Reina holding and consoling me. Again I was back before our Hawai'i days when, unable to accept the inevitability of death, I carried the curse of anxiety and dread. During an earlier bout, I had tried to come to terms with it through my novel *Ola*, examining the life of Finau and his approach to old age and death. I also realised halfway through writing the forty poems that make up the 'Garden' series of poems in *From Mānoa to a Ponsonby Garden* that I was doing the same there.

Reina and I have been together since 1991/92. I have been extremely fortunate in that she doesn't brood about past wrongs; she doesn't blame or find guilt; she doesn't live in her head in a future that is rife with danger and things going wrong. She lives in the present and is the most gifted multi-tasker I've ever known. She heals, and instead of feeling overwhelmed by what she has to do, she gets on with it. It's remarkable because not long after we became a partnership, she had to 'adopt' her three grandsons, her only son's children, and raise them while she was teaching full time at university. The mokopuna were two, three and five at the time.

Garden 40

A gumbooted Reina glows in the unexpected morning radiance

as she weeds the vegetable beds and turns over the soil with a trowel

My back my back! she complains but doesn't stop

She's cleaned the worm farm and collected the rich dark liquid from it

She'll use that to fertilise the beds before she plants the new vegetables

We were in a second-storey apartment in Mānoa so we couldn't have a garden

We couldn't have a cat either because of apartment regulations

But since our return to Ponsonby Reina has cultivated this garden

in which insects birds worms and other creatures the light and dark

the warmth and cold visitors Mānoa and I flourish

Out of it too has grown these poems in praise of Reina's gifted hands

and the friends and āiga who have died during the circle of the seasons

Songs in praise of the mauli which holds all things true to their search

and our journey from Mānoa to this Ponsonby garden

From Mānoa to a Ponsonby Garden (2012)

Now, once again, she had to try to cope with my rising depression and anxiety, and outbursts of anger and frustration. And for the first time she began to insist that I see a psychologist. In my whole life I'd never been to one, and wasn't planning to. I was of that macho generation who believed we could solve our own emotional and psychological problems. Like many other Samoan men my physical pain threshold is very high; when asked by my doctor about how high any of my pain was I'd say 4 or 5 on a scale of 10. Reina got so frustrated with my 'lying' about my pain that she told me off. 'How can doctors help you if you lie about your pain?'

What finally blew my mix of anxiety and dread to almost unbearable levels was facing my saofa'i, my title-bestowal ceremony, in Samoa. I'd had endless doubts about this since returning to Auckland from Samoa, having to prepare for the ceremony, and then going through with it. I was trapped again in terrible scenarios my tumultuous thoughts and imagination were conjuring up. Even my family doctor advised that I see a psychologist, and gave me a name and phone number.

I had two weekly sessions with the female psychologist before I went to Samoa for my saofa'i. And four when I returned.

She was a total stranger but open to discussing whatever I wanted. Immediately on talking with her, I lost most of my reservations. I could discuss things I couldn't discuss with people I knew well. Because she knew little about me – mainly what she'd read, heard and seen on TV – she could question me about things people who knew me would take for granted.

I found it healing to talk with a total stranger. It opened up new ways of looking at my anxieties and seeing them merely as doom scenarios that were never going to eventuate; that my survival mechanism, which made me anticipate any possible threats, was overreacting, over-imagining, over-thinking. And my condition was not unique: hundreds suffered from it. She suggested simple ways for me to bypass those scenarios. For instance, whenever my mind was over-worrying, I should concentrate on pleasurable images and memories of situations and things I'd loved. And I would tell my mind that most of the dire scenarios it was conjuring up were ridiculous. She gave me a list of exercises that would create a gap between me and the anxiety.

1. AN UNRELIABLE STORY?

Apart from the observation that the autobiography I'm writing is going to be a strange mix of some contradictions, asides and tangents, anecdotes, readings, raves and largely unsubstantiated claims, I want to think of it as the construction of a written and oral brew of what I was, am and will be in the ever-moving present.

Take note of the word *some*: like any other autobiography, mine is a highly selective, self-censored and unreliable story. And I'm not going to use my old age to excuse that! Don't trust me, be suspicious. I'm deliberately leaving out most of the story – it's none of your business, and I don't want to hurt the people I love. And my becoming in this autobiography depends on where and what I am at any time in that process. For instance, the autobiography is written from the viewpoint of a seventy-five-year-old whose body is disintegrating; an old-fashioned socialist who has watched, with angry disillusionment, the welfare state being dismantled over the last few decades; a grandfather who was not a very good father and who now, in turning white and arthritic and bionic, wants to be loved and forgiven and adored by his children and mokopuna.

It is going to be only a small part of my journey from the Vaipe, the Deadwater, but it will show how what I absorbed from its miraculous water has continued to influence my life to where I am now, Ponsonby.

INTO THE TUPUAGA

Our individual journeys are a process of discovering where we have come from, constructing, discarding, inventing, dreaming and then redoing it all in relation to what we discover at epiphanic moments of crisis or revelation in our lives. But most of us arrive at where we are at any given time without meaning to. Or as Arona, one of the main characters in my novel *The Mango's Kiss*, says:

Not many of us end up where we intend our selves to be at any given stage in our miserable lives. Look at me: when I left Samoa I intended to explore the Seven Seas and the papalagi world, becoming a devout Christian captain commanding my own defiant ship and returning triumphant to my loving aiga. An alcoholic Dutchman in one of my crews once said that we are our circumstances and the choices we made – or should've made but didn't ... Most of us end up where we are and who we are without meaning to. Profound, eh?

The Mango's Kiss (2003)

Arona's parents wanted him to be a pastor; he wanted to be a great sea captain but turned out to be a gangster without meaning to.

We assume that our children, through a natural process of osmosis, learn our histories of aiga, region and country without our teaching them. I suppose in pre-Papalagi Samoa, in the pre-European world, where educating the young was part of everyday life, you could say that was so to some extent. But I was born in 1939 into a society already saddled with a formal colonial education system where you actually went to a school, a place separate from your home and set up especially for that purpose.

The school was called Leifi'ifi School, established by the New Zealand administration exclusively for their children and other 'Europeans'. Because we have a German surname, the Wendts were considered 'European' and able to enrol in Leifi'ifi. Many of our 'non-European' cousins adopted our surname and were able to enrol as well. In that school little was taught of our indigenous ways of life. The culture of the coloniser was substituted for ours. So I ended up knowing little about pre-Papalagi Samoa. What I knew I learned from listening and watching our elders, especially my remarkable grandmother Mele and Aunt Ita, my father's oldest sister. Much later in life, when I attended university, I researched and learned much more.

So looking back at my writing life, you can say it has been a process of learning, through my writing, the depths of Samoan history and culture; the writing has been an attempt to discover it and to shape it my own way.

You can also say it has been a process of reading, researching and viewing, from my first remembered memory to now. I believe that my first remembered memory is:

Around her suddenly, the warm familiar smell of the man she'd later come to know as her father, and, as usual, she moved into it, letting it envelop her like a second skin. Down-pressing round coldness on her right cheek, radiating out across her face and down through her body to her tingling toes. She jerked away from it, hands clasped to the wet spot on her cheek. In her father's hand, at the centre of her seeing, was a round green-orange object. (A mango, she'd learn later.) From the object to his hand, to his face, she looked, recognising he was smiling. She moved closer to him, her hand taking the object, the fruit, which assumed the shape of her grip: solid, fitting, apt, balanced. Her father nuzzled his forehead against hers.

The Mango's Kiss

All the books I've read, all the films and TV I've seen, all that I've heard, from my mother singing the lullaby I first recognised as a song, that is the sum total of my experience. This book is about how that has infiltrated my writing, and how I've deliberately selected from my life's experience for my work, and how in that process I've learned how to explore further the real world and the world of the imagination – if there is such a thing. The total sum of your work is a mirror of your life that helps you to read your life – but is not your life. Or, as I've said before: we are what we remember or want to remember, the rope that stretches across the abyss of all that we've forgotten. Even what we remember becomes a story, a deliberate, ordered sequence that gives meaning to our lives. For we are all shit scared of having no meaning or worth.

What we prefer to omit is just as important as what we include. The actions we meant to take but didn't are as important as those taken. They are in the Va, the space between, which holds everything together in the Va-Atoa, the Unity-that-is-All.

Whenever I've looked back at my work, over

the past fifty years or so, I've been surprised by the constancy with which I've used my growing knowledge of things Samoan, especially of pre-Papalagi Samoa. And as I've discovered and imagined and created my own version of that world, I've used that in my new work. From my first collection of short stories, *Flying-Fox in a Freedom Tree*, through my first novel, *Sons for the Return Home*, to *Pouliuli*, *Leaves of the Banyan Tree*, and even to my futuristic novel, *Black Rainbow*, and my latest novel, *The Adventures of Vela*, that holds true. When Arona, the son of the Aiga Sa-Tuifolau, dies tragically in New Zealand in *The Mango's Kiss*, his sister, Peleiupu, brings his ashes back to Samoa. Their family bury him secretly in the Aiga Sa-Tuifolau's secret burial place, Niuafei, that began with their aiga's pagan Atua Fatutapu, and where his father, the staunch Christian pastor, insists that he too be buried.

Throughout my work, the spiritual world of ancient Samoa that was banned by the missionaries – and is still banned by the Christians today – lives and grows and is respected. That world is now appearing in the work of other Samoan and Pacific writers and artists. Art ain't life, but for me it's a way of resurrecting our atua and reconstituting reality.

So I want to open with:

Le Tupuaga

I le Amataga na'o Tagaloaalagi lava
Na soifua i le Vānimonimo
Na'o ia lava
Leai se Lagi, leai se Lau'ele'ele
Na'o ia lava na soifua i le Vānimonimo
O ia na faia mea uma lava
I le tūlaga na tū ai Tagaloaalagi
Na ola mai ai le Papa
Ma na sāunoa atu Tagaloa i le Papa, 'Pā loa'
Ma ua fānau mai Papata'oto
Soso'o ai ma Papasosolo
Ma Papalaua'au ma isi Papa ese'ese
Ta e Tagaloa i lona lima taumatau le Papa
Fānau mai Ele'ele, le Tamā o Tagata
Na fānau mai ai fo'i Sami lea ua sosolo
I luga o Papa uma lava
Taga'i atu Tagaloa i lona itū taumatau
Ola mai le vai
Toe sāunoa o ia i le Papa, 'Pā loa'
Fānau mai Tuite'elagi ma Ilu
Ma Mamao, le Tama'ita'i
Ma niuao, ma Luaao, le Tama
Na fa'apēnā ona fausia e Tagaloaalagi
Mea uma lava
Seia o'o ina fānau mai Tagata, Loto,
Atamai, Finagalo, ma Masalo
Na i'u ai i'inā le fānau a Tagaloa ma le Papa

In the Beginning there was only Tagaloaalagi
Living in the Vānimonimo
Only He
No sky, no land
Only He in the Vānimonimo
He created Everything
Out of where He stood
Grew the Papa
Tagaloa said to the Papa, Give birth!
And Papataoto was born
And then Papasosolo
And Papalaua'au and other different Papa
With His right hand Tagaloa struck the Papa
And Ele'ele was born, the Father of Humankind
And Sea was also born to cover
All the Papa
Tagaloa looked to His right
And Water was born
He said to Papa, Give birth!
And Tuite'elagi and Ilu were born
And Mamao, the Woman,
And Niuao, and Lua'ao, the Son
In that manner Tagaloa created
Everything else
Until Tagata, Loto,
Atamai, Finagalo, and Masalo were born
There ended the children of Tagaloaalagi and the Papa

The Songmaker's Chair (2004)

Tupuaga literally means ways of growing, origins or how and where things grow from. The above version of the Tupuaga was recorded by the London Missionary Society missionary George Pratt from two tu'ua, keepers of the knowledge.

It is interesting that in the Beginning there is only Tagaloaalagi, the Supreme Creator, existing in the Vanimonimo, the Space-that-appears-and-disappears, and that it is from where He stood that the first Papa, the Rock, grows. And it is that Rock that He orders to give birth. The myth has some 'scientific' truth in that volcanic islands came out of fire and molten lava, and solidified lava (the Rock) eventually breaks down into eleele, soil, earth. (Our words for blood and soil are the same: toto, eleele and palapala. So when you bleed you are bleeding earth, soil.) Then Tagaloaalagi created water, the source of all life, which covers and 'mates' with the various types of rocks, which in turn give birth to other elements and creatures.

Growing up in Samoa we were never told this genesis narrative because it was considered 'pagan', belonging to the Aso o le Fa'apaupau ma le Pogisa, the Days of Paganism and Darkness. Even our beloved grandmother Mele, who had enormous respect for that banned knowledge, did not tell us. We were fed on the Christian Genesis every evening lotu and Sunday service, and at pastor's school. Once in a fale-aitu, we watched a faifaleaitu parodying part of the Tupuaga, playing on what he (and his fundamentalist Christian audience) deemed the hilarious incredibility of atua mating with rocks that then begat other rocks. It wasn't until the 1960s while I was researching the Mau movement that I came across a written version of the Tupuaga, but I didn't think it important to my life then.

When I was Director of the University of the South Pacific Centre in Apia from 1976 to the middle of 1982, our historians Malama and Penny Meleisea and I received money from the UNESCO Pacific Cultural Project to finance the writing of the first history of Samoa by Samoans. We decided to begin the history with the Tupuaga: a bold declaration that our history was *our* history and was to be told *our* way, respecting oral history and traditions and our indigenous beginnings as much as Christians believe that in the Beginning was the Word and the Word was God ...

And as I thought about the meanings of the Tupuaga, it began to root itself deeper in my psyche. I would find over the years that as I learned more, through my research and writing about the pagan Samoan world, that knowledge and the atua and aitu and other beings who inhabited that world would assume compelling presences in my writing and imagination and dreaming.

In the late 1990s, when I decided to write my first full-length play, *The Songmaker's Chair*, I made those atua the heart and soul of the play. The play opens with them at the back and edges, at the periphery; but by the end, they are at the stage front, carrying the body of Peseola, the Head of the Aiga Sa-Peseola, away to Pulotu, the spirit world. In the play there is no difference between the Christian God and the atua of Samoa.

While I was revising the play, I was advised that it was too didactic, and that I should cut out most of the historical, cultural and anthropological information in it. I ignored that advice, and used the play to teach our young people and non-Samoan audiences about our ancient religion and beliefs. I think it worked with most audiences. I was also keeping true to the traditions of Samoan storytelling, to the way knowledge and values were handed on.

The Songmaker's Chair took me seven years to write and get onto the stage. It was first performed in the first Auckland Arts Festival in September 2003, directed by my cousin Nathaniel Lees; he also played Peseola. The play sold out for its long season, and received standing ovations.

For me, it was moving, emotionally uplifting and so joyously fulfilling to watch our young moko really enjoying the play. They were sitting with Reina while I hid and watched from the corner –

some of them even jumped to their feet and joined the rap being performed by the actors.

When it played in Hawai'i, it also sold out.

I was especially moved by the enthusiastic reactions of the New Zealand-born Samoan and Pasefika audiences. As one of them said to me: 'I loved it because it is about my grandparents and parents. It's the first time I've seen their lives on the stage. And it is about being Samoan in another country. I've also learned much from it about our religion, beliefs, and ancestors.'

LAVA AND THE FAFA

I was about ten when my grandmother and Aunt Mine, with a group of able young men, took me on a malaga round Savai'i to visit relatives. In those days there were no roads round much of Savai'i. We had to walk across the lava fields, and the young men took turns piggybacking me across.

Years later I would describe the impact of those fields and the lava on my being:

'…This world that people believe they want so much is only true in the movies because people make the movies. You get me?' says Tagata. I shake the head. 'Okay, well let me explain it this way,' he continues. 'Have you seen the lava fields in Savaii?' I shake the head again. 'Two years ago I went there with some friends. You travel for miles through forest and so many villages where people have ruined the beauty, and then … . And then It is there. You feel you are right in it at last. Get me? Like you are there where the peace lies, where all the dirty little places and lies and monuments we make to our selves mean nothing because lava can be nothing else but lava. You get me?' He stops for a while and looks at me. 'The lava spreads for miles right into the sea. Nothing else. Just black silence like the moon maybe. You remember that movie us guys saw years ago? Well, it looks like that, like the moon surface in that movie. A flood of lava everywhere. But in some places you see small plants growing through the cracks in the lava, like funny stories breaking through your stony mind. Get me? I felt like I have been searching for that all my miserable life. Boy, it made me see things so clear for once. That being a dwarf or a giant or a saint does not mean anything.' Tagata's eyes glow brightly. 'That we are all equal in the silence, in the nothing, in lava. I did not want to leave the lava fields, but ... but then you cannot stay there forever because you will die of thirst and hunger if you stay. There is no water, no food, just lava. All is lava.'

'Flying-Fox in a Freedom Tree', in
Flying-Fox in a Freedom Tree (1974)

At the western tip of the island of Savai'i in Falealupo and Tufutafoe is the Fafa-o-Sauali'i, the point where the spirits depart for Pulotu, the Spirit World. The sun sets directly opposite the Fafa. When you die your agaga, soul, journeys to the Fafa where it bathes in the pool on the beach and then takes the lava tunnel into the sea and down into Pulotu.

Falealupo was also the centre of the Atua Nafanua, the War Goddess, and Her religion, which ruled Samoa for the 300 years before Christianity arrived.

That visit to the lava fields and the Fafa-o-Sauali'i had a radical effect on me. Later, whenever I returned from boarding school and university in New Zealand, I always tried to visit the Fafa and the lava fields. For me it was a pilgrimage, always with an intuitive sense of respect, alofa or love, and awe tinged with a bone-deep fear of the presences of the ancient taulaaitu and the Atua Nafanua, who were feared throughout Samoa. After the conversion of the Falealupoans to Catholicism, the Fafa was left to grow over with forest, creepers and palms. I loved entering that cool green sanctuary and simply sitting on the beach and watching the lava tunnel, imagining the agaga making their journey into the sea and Pulotu.

Lava and the Fafa became central and recurring symbols in my work. They find their major expression in my novel *The Adventures of Vela* (2009), which has Nafanua at its core.

In 2000 the world, including Samoa, celebrated the millennium. I heard that Tufutafoe and Falealupo and the Fafa were being 'prepared' for those celebrations.

A year after the millennium celebrations, Reina and I drove off the main road and down to Falealupo and Tufutafoe and the Fafa.

The villages looked new, renovated, clean. We drove into the Point and through the Fafa without realising it. I was disoriented because the forest had been cleared and three spacious orderly fale stood by the road near the beach.

We stopped, and a man came out to us. I asked him where the Fafa was, and he smiled and said we were right there: it would cost us $10 to park our car and use one of the fale and picnic on the beach. He also said we could swim in the pool on the beach. In English I told Reina that the pool was the sacred one in which the agaga cleansed themselves before their final journey. I could tell from the expression in her eyes there was no way she was going to desecrate that pool. You can take pictures too, the man said, smiling. I realised this was a preparation for the tourist tsunami that they believed would come with the celebrations of the millennium.

Such contradictions of history include the fact that one of my granddaughters, Sina Nafanua, is a direct descendant of the Aiga Sa-Auva'a, one of the two taulaaitu, or priestly, families of Nafanua. Auva'a and Tupa'i, Nafanua's taulaaitu, led Her armies and fought Her wars and acquired for Her all the Tafa'ifa titles, the most important titles of

Samoa. From being a minor war god and a woman, Auva'a and Tupa'i turned Nafanua and Her religion into the most powerful force in Samoa, for 300 years, before the Christian missionaries came.

Even today whenever the Auva'a title falls vacant and the Aiga Sa-Auva'a chooses a replacement, if anything dire happens to that person, people say that Nafanua is showing Her displeasure with their choice.

Nafanua and our ancient beliefs and religion live, woven even into the way we practise Christianity. Nafanua can't be destroyed because the genealogies of the Aiga of Falealupo and Tufutafoe are anchored to Her; to destroy Her would be to erase the most important strand of their genealogy that connects them to their lands and titles. So on one level those aiga try to dismiss Her as part of the pagan Darkness but are afraid of Her because She can destroy them. On a deeper level, they know they are unimportant without Her because it was She who acquired all the Tafa'ifa titles of Samoa and made Falealupo central to the whole genealogy of Samoa and its sacred Aiga. Genetically, they are also Her descendants.

These contradictions are the stuff of life in Samoa; they propel, govern and compel our sight and determine our emotional, psychological and spiritual behaviour. This, of course, is not new wherever different cultures meet, intermingle or clash. Our lives in the present are layers of maps created by that process:

I called the City Council offices and got maps of the city delivered immediately. We spread them out on the dining table ...

Using the maps, they took me block by block, street by street, through the inner city. Names of businesses, buildings, places, gossip about those, recent happenings, some history, stories of crimes and daring deeds they'd committed against those people and places. They even filled in what wasn't in the maps, especially when we descended into the labyrinth below the inner city, into a world I knew nothing about. Sewage systems, tunnels, communication and power links and lines, forgotten byways and drains, nooks and crannies they used as home, as safehouses. A city underneath a city, holding it up. 'A city is layers of maps and geographies, layers of them, centuries of it. We were the first, our ancestors, no matter what lies the Tribunal says. So our maps are at the bottom of the bloody heap. They're still there though the bloody otherworlders have tried to fucking well erase them. As long as we survive ... ' Manu said.

Black Rainbow (1992)

Contradictions were also built into us by the Atua Tagaloaalagi. In Samoan mythology, when the Supreme Atua, Tagaloaalagi, created us and our islands, He gifted us agaga (soul), poto (cunning, wit), masalo (doubt), loto (spirit), atamai (intelligence) and fingalo (will). Those marvellous gifts make for contradiction: they make us capable not only of enormous love and creativity, healing and invention, but also of arrogance, cruelty and violence. That contradiction is at the heart of all our cultures, philosophies and literatures. I grew up in the latter half of the twentieth century, a time of incredible invention in technology and science and the arts, yet also a time of horrific violence and suffering, brutality and injustice. Everywhere we look today we see a tragic continuation of that. We are cannibalising ourselves and our planet to death.

LE VA AND FOLAUGA

In the Samoan view of reality all things, both animate and inanimate, are related through the Va, the space between that holds them together. We are connected to other creatures, trees, stones, the environment, the atua and the universe in the Va-Atoa, the Unity-that-is-All. Everything is related in va-feiloa'i, relationships of mutual respect and balance. That connectedness is holistic, so to alter any part of it alters the whole Unity, re-transfigures it.

When the two-lettered va is added to or appears in another word, it transforms and deepens the meaning of that word or term. For instance, our word vasa means ocean. Va = space, sa = forbidden or sacred. So vasa means the space that is forbidden and sacred. When that becomes Vasa Loloa, it becomes the sacred space that is long and ancient, the Pacific Ocean.

When the term va is added to our term mana (the power essence of someone or something), it becomes the term manava, meaning stomach, or breath. Our language is full of such words.

The self is defined in terms of itu (sides) and in the va, your connections to the group: tatou (us), outou (you), aiga (family), nu'u (village), itumalo (district), atunu'u (country). You define o a'u (yourself, or me) in terms of your gafa or genealogy. You also define yourself in terms of the itu fa'aletino (physical side), le itu fa'aleagaga (spiritual side), le itu fa'aleaiga (your family side), le itu fa'aleitumalo (your relationships to the district). Your gafa includes your relationships to your ancestors and atua, and everything else.

So a nu'u, or village, is made up of a group of aiga, or extended families. Those aiga are connected through history and gafa. Village aiga, in turn, are connected to other aiga in other villages and districts throughout Samoa. At the national level, aiga are grouped in the important aiga of Samoa: the Aiga Sa-Tupua and the Aiga Sa-Malietoa. The present Head of State, Tui Atua Tupua Tamasese Taisi Efi is the highest Ali'i, Tamaaiga, of the Aiga Sa-Tupua.

You can belong to all the aiga you are connected to through marriage, history and genealogy. All aiga have genealogies that extend back to our atua. In our pre-Christian religion, each aiga had a family atua. My aiga's was the Lulu, the Owl. I still remember that, when I was a boy while were accompanying our grandmother Mele to our plantation in Malie one morning, we came across the body of a dead owl beside the track. Our grandmother immediately squatted down beside the bird and started wailing as if someone had died; she scratched her face as well. Puzzled and afraid, we watched her wrap up the body in banana leaves, and we had to dig a hole in which she buried the owl. She never told us why, but one of our aunts told us later that the Owl had been our family's atua.

Districts or itumalo also had atua, such as the Fe'e (Octopus), the Atua-loa (Centipede), the Gogosina (Long-tailed Tropic Bird) and others. There were also atua of the sea, the forests, the sky, thunder and lightning, war, and so forth. Each aiga's atua included atua-tagata – half-god/half-human – who were born of relationships between atua and humans. All the atua were organised in a hierarchical structure, with the Supreme Atua, Tagaloaalagi, at the top. He created everything, as I've explained.

The district and national atua had taulaaitu,

priests, who served them. I've already talked about Nafanua and her taulaaitu, Auva'a and Tupa'i.

The centre of our ancient religion was Manu'a, in eastern Samoa. And the head of it was the Tuimanu'a, the Ali'i Paia, the most sacred of our priests and Tamaaiga.

You have to know your gafa because they are a major strand in defining who and what you are, and where you originated. You should also know them so that you can prove your claim to your aiga titles, house sites and land. Whenever there are disputes about land and titles, each party has to appear before the Lands and Titles Court for the dispute to be settled. (The court was set up by the German colonial government to stop the wars and violent disputes that frequently erupted over titles and land.) Your court petition has to show how you are connected to the disputed title and how close that connection is. You have to prove your genealogical line to all the previous holders of that title. If you don't know your genealogy and history intimately, you will probably lose the case. The Lands and Titles Court is our most overworked court! Hundreds of cases wait to be heard every year. No lawyers are allowed into the court – petitioners have to represent themselves.

2. WHAT ARE MY TUPUAGA?

It is considered impolite and arrogant to discuss your gafa in public, but even worse is discussing the gafa of other aiga. Gafa are considered sacred. So I'll take the less presumptuous option and discuss mine to illustrate the points I am making. I'll try to sound modest!

On my father's side, one of my aiga is called Le Aiga Sa-Tuaopepe, a branch of the Aiga Sa-Su'a. The family is centred in the village of Gagaifo-o-le-Vao, Lefaga, and extends throughout Samoa and now overseas. My father held the Tuaopepe title and was the Ali'i of our aiga. A few years before he died, he handed his title to our brother Felix, who is still Tuaopepe today.

Again on my father's side, our main aiga is Le Aiga Sa-Maualaivao of Malie. The original Wendt, Ernst Wendt, came from Germany in the late nineteenth century and married Kuea, the sister of Maualaivao Fili of Malie, one of the main centres of the Aiga Sa-Malietoa. Their son Heinrich married Mele Trood, daughter of the then British consul, Thomas Trood. Her mother was of the Aiga Sa-Sao of the Aiga Sa-Malietoa of Sapapaali'i, Savai'i.

Because Maualaivao Fili didn't have children, his sister Kuea's children became his main heirs. Every Samoan Wendt you meet today is descended from that line.

Heinrich and Mele Wendt produced Ida, Otto, Henry, Mine and Rudy. Henry was my father.

While Mele was dying, at the age of ninety-three or ninety-five, we counted all her direct descendants: one hundred of them, the hundredth one being our second daughter whom my wife Jenny was carrying at the time. We called her Mele.

Our branch of the Aiga Sa-Maualaivao is known as the Suli-o-Maualaivao Fili, the-Heirs-of-Maualaivao Fili. Two of my cousins, sons of my Aunt Ida, held the Maualaivao title. Then the title on our side of the family was vacant for about ten years. Once our immediate aiga in Malie was quite large, but now only one sister, Lizzie, and her husband Lupi and their two teenage children are left. We decided to rebuild our aiga, and to do that properly we had to fill our vacant Maualaivao title. So three years ago, our branch of the Aiga Sa-Maualaivao met in Samoa to choose a successor.

I and many of my brothers and sisters, cousins and children came from around Samoa and the world for that meeting. After two days of discussions in our old family home in the Vaipe, we agreed to offer the title to our oldest brother, Taulapapa Hans/Anisi, who had retired to live in Samoa after spending over fifty years in America and becoming a successful businessman and banker.

He spent two sleepless nights in reflection and then turned it down, saying he was too old and insufficiently knowledgeable about things Samoan to accept the title and lead our family. He wanted me to take the title, and the majority of our aiga agreed with him.

So I spent two sleepless nights talking to Reina and my children and some friends. They told me I couldn't turn it down. For most of my adult life, I'd turned down offers from my different aiga to take a matai title. Because I'd lived away from Samoa for much of my life, they argued it was now my turn to contribute directly to the leadership of our aiga. My brother Taulapapa also wanted me to take the title. So I couldn't get out of it, despite my fears that I was too old, that I didn't particularly want to live in Samoa permanently, and that I wouldn't be able to fulfil my duties and responsibilities as the Maualaivao.

I said yes, and agreed with my aiga that my saofa'iga should take place as soon as possible.

I returned to Auckland and tried to forget about it. Then, about a year later, I had to return to Samoa for another fa'alavelave, the death of my brother Max, who was a retired police superintendent. After Max's funeral, some of the elders of my aiga reminded me, politely, about my saofa'i, that we couldn't delay it any more because some of our aiga's enemies were scheming and campaigning, in Malie, against my having the title. Reluctantly I agreed to having the saofa'i early the following year, 2012.

So, in mid-January 2012, many of our relatives and friends gathered in Samoa and Malie for my saofa'i. It was to be held on Saturday 28 January. Reina and I and my children and their spouses and children got there a week before to help in the preparations.

The Maualaivao title is one of the three highest ali'i in Malie and the district of the Vaimauga, so many people were looking for large gifts of money and ie toga (fine mats) from the saofa'i, and they manoeuvred the ceremony to achieve that. But we were raised by our frugal father to live within our means – and we weren't going to be conned by anyone.

When I lived in Samoa in the 1960s and 70s, I was involved in only a few saofa'i, usually to do with my aiga and friends, but I was never in the middle of one. This was my first time – and as usual my imagination was frightening me to death.

Since their return to live in Samoa my brother Hans and his wife Flora have become the centre and head of our aiga, alongside our brother Tuaopepe Felix/Fili and his wife Marita.

We refer to Taulapapa as 'the Banker', and Flora is the ablest manager of business and fa'alavelave we've ever worked with. She had organised my brother Max's funeral to perfection down to the last detail – it had been a splendid, tasteful, appropriately solemn affair, involving a full mass, and was attended by hundreds of aiga and friends.

After I had agreed to take the title, Hans and Flora dispelled many of my fears by promising they would organise my saofa'i.

With the help of some of her sisters and mine, and our children and some of the younger matai in our aiga, Flora organised the money, ie toga and food, enough for at least 500 people. My son Michael and other cousins and workers in Flora's company, along with our grandchildren, renovated and repainted and cleaned my cousin Seiuli Alualu's maota (meeting house), the venue for the saofa'i. Then, directed by Flora and the older women, they decorated the maota with mats, ie toga and siapo (tapa), and wove streams of flowers and coconut leaves round the posts and rafters. They also put up two voluminous tents in front of the maota to be used for seating other guests and as our headquarters for the public distribution of the ie toga, money and food.

Flora had puletasi, ie lavalava and shirts of the same material and design made for all our aiga who were to serve on the day. I stupidly asked why. Flora said: it's going to be a huge affair with hundreds of people milling around; we have to stop other people joining the servers and stealing things. Anyone who didn't have a uniform wouldn't be allowed to serve.

Early in the morning on Saturday 28 January 2012, we drove to our home in Vailoa, Malie, and waited there for the saofa'i to start at mid-morning, Reina dressed in a magnificent puletasi, which Flora had her dressmakers design and sew. I dressed in ie toga, with a whaletooth necklace and feather headwear, and was then oiled with coconut oil.

I was surprised at how calm, relaxed and certain I felt. It is always reassuring to have Reina with you: she views the world as a realist, and once you commit yourself to something, you have to do it. So what's the use of worrying? I was in this important unstoppable saofa'i, so go with the flow. If you're not enjoying it, she said, just observe all its intricacies, features, rituals and practices, and try to understand how the ceremony has developed in Samoa. You're also in the dead middle of it – the subject, the object and the verb! Our aiga and friends filled the eastern side of the maota, with me occupying the middle post and Taulapapa and

Tuaopepe on either side. The rest of our matai and aiga occupied the other posts.

We watched two long lines of the Malie matai, led by the ali'i and followed by the aumaga, filing from the middle of the village along the main road and then into the maota. They carried kava sticks.

The ali'i sat down opposite us across the fale. Three of them were part of the main opposition to my aiga. The other matai spread out round the posts according to their rank. The leading tulafale and aumaga lined up at the back of the fale, with the taupou and kava bowl. I recognised some of the matai whom I'd grown up with in the village but hadn't seen for decades.

The ceremonies opened with a hymn that filled the house and spread out into the light and over the mangroves and across the bay. The pastor – our family pastor but one who was married to a branch of our aiga that was trying to claim the Maualaivao title – read from the Bible, then sermonised for a while. I knelt in front of him and, laying his hand on my head, he asked God to bless my saofa'i and my life and new responsibilities as the Maualaivao. There was another hymn and a prayer.

Our orator thanked the pastor, who then left. The affairs of God must not be mixed with those from the past and of this world!

Other ceremonies followed – the ava ceremony, the fa'atau and lauga, and then the distribution of the ava. I enjoyed watching and participating, because the ceremonies were carried out with meticulous care and proper observation of the correct rituals and practices, as well as with flair, finesse and love. It was epic theatre; it was poetry.

Then our aiga reciprocated with the distribution of money and ie toga, which continued until all the matai of Malie and from elsewhere were satisfied with their shares.

The elaborate lunch was then served.

We hired a video team to film all that day's events – a valuable record for students and researchers and for my family to learn from.

My family and I then returned to New Zealand. A few months later, after my brother Tuaopepe Fili registered my title in the Lands and Titles Court, some of the ali'i and matai who had participated in my saofa'i lodged petitions against my right to hold the Maualaivao title.

The court hearing took place months later. But that's another story for another hot day in Paradise. It's enough to say that we won the court case.

THE MIX

On my mother's side, I am of le Aiga Sa-Patu of Vaiala and le Aiga Sa-Asi of Moata'a. My mother was Luisa Patu, and her father, my grandfather, was Patu Togi, son of Asi Tunupopo of Moata'a. Her mother was Amy Fruean. Two Fruean brothers, from an

American Jewish family, married into our aiga Sa-Su'a in Lefaga. Amy Fruean, my grandmother, was a descendant.

Throughout our history, Samoan aiga have always intermarried with other ethnic groups, despite the claim by many of us that we are Samoan only if we are 'full-blooded Samoan' (whatever that means). Even our Tamaaiga are not 'full-blooded Samoans'. Measuring one's authenticity by blood quantum came with the colonisers and their ideas about race. Ranking people according to their degree of 'pure' blood meant that 'mixed blood' families like ours came to be seen as 'inferior'. We were called 'half-castes', afakasi.

But I was born the same mix that Samoa has always been – a society that has always incorporated the outside world, since long before the European colonisers arrived. Though we lived in Apia, the capital and only town in Samoa, my father, as ali'i, was responsible for the welfare of our aiga throughout Samoa and abroad. He had to attend fono with our aiga matai in Lefaga whenever it was necessary; Lefaga matai came regularly to Apia to consult him or ask for help; whenever relatives and Lefaga villagers visited Apia they usually stayed with us (sometimes we had to house and feed hundreds); whenever children of our Lefaga aiga needed to come to school in Apia, they stayed with us, and our parents paid for their education and cared for them as if they were their own children. When relatives wanted to migrate, our father usually helped finance their journeys.

Fa'alavelave is an inescapable term if you're Samoan. Fa'a means to make, lavalave means an entanglement. So a fa'alavelave is something that entangles you, an 'entanglement' – such as a wedding, funeral, a church-village project, a title-bestowal ceremony, a birthday (especially a twenty-first), and so on. And if you want to be considered an ideal matai, member of a family, church, village, you have to contribute to these fa'alavelave generously and without complaining. The amount and size of your contribution (which is always publicly displayed) should reflect the size of your rank.

So my Dad, being the head of our aiga, and one of the highest ranking ali'i in Lefaga, was expected to contribute the most. And we his children who had jobs contributed to his contribution. When it came to money, my father, who grew up in poverty and had to work extremely hard to build up his plumbing business, was very shrewd and frugal. He often berated our aiga at length for being 'foolishly extravagant and show-offish Samoans' – then gave them what they wanted. Our aiga referred to him, affectionately but behind his plumber's back, as the 'Sifi Siamagi', the German Chief.

Our father expected us to contribute according to our means and voluntarily. He was unusual in this. Other aiga, according to the fa'asamoa, expected their members to contribute according to their rank, and it was compulsory.

So in our aiga, my sisters, brothers and I, because we earned the most money, contributed the money that was needed. Other aiga members contributed ie toga, food and labour. When our father died, we organised his funeral and aiga contributions to it according to the tradition he had established.

3. LE VAIPE, THE DEADWATER

We are not people of Apia, yet when I was born my aiga was living in Tauese, a suburb of Apia. My grandfather, Tuaopepe Tauilo, and grandmother, Mele, had shifted to Apia so he could participate in the Mau movement of the 1920s. He bought almost 1 acre of land in Tauese from one of the ali'i of Apia.

The main reason why he agreed to shift to town was this: the movement for self-government had erupted and Apia was alive and invigoratingly pregnant with forebodings of violent action and political intrigue, things so essential to grandfather's spiritual health. He also saw the movement as a god-given opportunity to prove once and for all to his enemies that he was a great orator and freedom fighter and nationalist leader.

'Pint-size Devil on a Thoroughbred',
in *Flying-Fox in a Freedom Tree*

So because our Lefaga grandfather wanted to be in the Mau, the movement for self-government, our aiga found itself in the Vaipe, Apia.

The name Vaipe, Deadwater, is a neighbourhood name for our little neighbourhood; outside it is known as Tauese. We named it after the small brackish stream that flows through the community, a swampy stream in a swampy, boggy area. The stream was strong when I was growing up, but with the building of more houses and fale, and with drainage and roading over the years, it has weakened considerably and now flows through large drain pipes; it flash floods only when we have heavy rain and high tides.

As children, fascinated by the English language and movies, we referred to the little stream as our 'Mississippi'. When I meet my sisters and brothers and our friends from that childhood today, we all laugh and refer to it as the Mississippi!

The Vaipe has the Roman Catholic Cathedral at its western boundary, the court and police station to the east, the market and harbour in front, and the swamps behind it. These are convenient boundaries that I've turned into a symbolic fence for the marvellous world of the Deadwater. Inside that, I've established my aiga's 'God's Little Acre'.

In that God's Little Acre over the years we have had three fale, a small store, and a double-storeyed Palagi house, which my father built in the 1960s.

In my childhood there were always at least forty people living in that compound: my parents and ten of us, my Aunt Mine and Uncle Taulauati and their children, and, on and off, other aunts and uncles and their siblings, and the children of relatives from the villages. It was extremely difficult for my parents to feed, clothe and educate everyone, and also to contribute to the innumerable fa'alavelave.

Because my mother was a nofotane – meaning she had married into the family – the Wendts, especially my father's sisters and brothers, expected her to play a secondary role. This proved to be the domestic task of organising and, with the younger family members, doing all the chores. The haunting memory of my mother hand washing the laundry of that number of people under the cold tap in the outside shower, soaping the clothes and then pounding them with a wooden pounder, and then hand-wringing them, morning after morning, has remained with me to this day.

We didn't have a fridge, inside kitchen or stove, so all the cooking was done outside over an open fire in our umu faleo'o. We all had to wash and shower under the shower outside under gatae trees.

So on a typical week day, those who were rostered to do the cooking got up earlier than the others. The rest of us got up at six, had lotu with our grandmother, then went outside to pick up the rubbish. We washed our faces in the outside shower, dried them with the one towel we had to share, dressed for school, and then had breakfast comprising of two slices of buttered bread (and jam if lucky), and a cup of sugared tea.

School started at 8; we walked there. No lunch. We returned home when school finished at 1 p.m. In the early days of the Vaipe, when our parents couldn't afford lunch, we had to wait for the final evening meal to eat again. That meal was usually a large stew or supo of mutton flaps or tinned fish, and boiled green bananas. We all looked forward to the to'ona'i on Sunday, the main lunch of the week, when like every other family we cooked an umu and enjoyed larger helpings of a greater variety of food. To this day, I still remember what feeling hungry for long periods of time is like. I have to remember, though, that most other families in Samoa, especially in the urban area, were like us.

Our grandmother refused to live in the Palagi house. We, the children, spent most of our time in her spacious fale, which before our Palagi house was built in the 1960s was our family home. Nearly all the children and older siblings slept there communally under large mosquito nets.

Every evening, we gathered for the family lotu, conducted by our father. He would open the service by welcoming everyone. Then our mother, who had a marvellous soprano voice, started singing a hymn and we would all join her in four-part harmony. Our father would then read from the Bible – or choose someone else to do so. He would then talk about the reading, and use it to chastise us for anything wrong we'd done that day.

Years after my grandmother's death, while I was home for a visit, my father asked me to say the prayer. Everyone in our aiga knew I was no longer a church-goer – a major sin in Samoan terms. And they all knew he had me cornered, but they had forgotten that I was no longer the obedient, reticent son. I simply looked across at my father and declared, politely, it would be best if someone who still believed said the prayer; I even asked one of my younger brothers to say it. Over the next few years my father and aiga came to accept my atheism: they knew I wasn't ever going to repent and return to the Christian fold.

Then, after the family meal, we showered and gathered in our grandmother's fale. She would ask for volunteers to ku'i (pound) her legs, and while the volunteers did this as she lay under her blanket, her head on her ali, she would tell us fagogo – myths and legends. We would lie on sleeping mats in our nets, listening.

This tradition of fagogo telling in the evenings is an ancient one. Elders who are the keepers of these fagogo do the storytelling in a set format. Fagogo are used to hand down values, genealogies, moral lessons, histories, beliefs and ways of viewing the world.

Our grandmother was the best fagogo-teller in the Vaipe and Apia, so many of the neighbourhood children often turned up as well. In the quiet of the nets and fale, with the air drenched with the smell of the Vaipe, we lay waiting, eagerly, for her to start.

'Sa i ai le ulugali'i o Fau ma Ogafau,' her deep captivating voice came out of the dark. 'Nonofo, nonofo Fau ma Ogafau maua le la tama, o Tasi. Toe nonofo, nonofo Fau ma Ogafau maua le teine o Sina … There was a couple called Fau and Ogafau. They lived and lived together and begot a son called Tasi. Then they lived and lived and begot a daughter named Sina …' She would first establish the location and the main characters and then weave the tale, the narrative, the adventure, and take us with her in the ways she paced her telling.

A fagogo includes a tagi, a chorus, which the storyteller will make you memorise before she tells her tale. When Mele sensed we were falling asleep or not listening, she would stop the tale and say, 'Tagi mai le fagogo,' 'Chant me the tagi.' And we had to chant the tagi. If we sounded sleepy or unenthusiastic, she would make us repeat the tagi.

Her fagogo ranged from ancient myths and legends that explained the creation of the world and Samoa and humans, to tales of mythical adventurers such as Ti'eti'e-a-talaga, to frightening ghost stories. And then she would dazzle us with Grimm's stories, Greek mythology and Aesop's tales – which we believed at the time were of her own making. (Later, at boarding school, I found collections of Aesop's fables and Grimm's fairy tales in the school library and recognised the stories she'd told us in Samoan in her unique way as fagogo.)

Because she was bilingual, she would unexpectedly swing into English, and have us scrambling to understand what she was saying. She'd chortle and ask, 'Anyone know what I just said?' And we'd all rush to translate.

She taught me early how to pace and narrate a story to hold your audience's attention. I also learned that a story is only 'true' if in the telling you can *persuade* your listeners it is true. And basic to that is creating memorable characters who are usually larger than life, and having a plot line that unravels mystery and, in so doing, adds to our understanding of who and what we are.

All my writing life I've submitted my poems, essays, stories, novels to my grandmother's critical judgement and orality. Each piece must work for me orally: if I read it aloud and it doesn't 'fit' my throat, I rewrite and rewrite it – until I hear my grandmother chortling her approval.

FA'AMAFU

The Vaipe was a rich mix of fundamentalist Christianity (everyone went to church and the only book in most of our homes was the Bible), ancient Samoa and the Tivoli Theatre world of films.

It was also notorious for illegal home-brewing and prostitution, which was never referred to in public as that. In colonial Samoa you had to get a license from the police to buy liquor from the government customs store, the only liquor outlet in the country. And only 'Europeans' and high-ranking Samoans who were granted liquor licenses could buy and consume alcohol. So thirsty unlicensed Samoans had to produce their own or buy it secretly from illegal brewers. The homebrew was called fa'amafu, the fermented.

Our neighbours just over the hibiscus hedge to the west were amongst Apia's leading brewers. They brewed and fermented their fa'amafu at night, bottled it and then, for the beer to age hidden from the police, they shelved the bottles in the thatched dome of their main fale or buried them in the swamps behind us. The Faualo children were some of our closest friends, so we sometimes helped with bottling and burying the brew, without our parents knowing.

Next to their fale was a two-storeyed Palagi house built for the purpose of entertaining Palagi sailors and other customers. Downstairs was for partying and drinking the homebrew. Upstairs was for 'things between men and women we shouldn't know about', as one of the Faualo boys described it.

The first Papalagi and other foreigners we ever saw up close were those who came to enjoy those pleasures and the Faualos' hospitality. So our first impression of Papalagi was that they had lots of money, loved parties, and were always drunk, noisy and easy to divest of their money and other belongings, including their clothes.

Needless to say, police raids on the house and fale took place frequently. Mostly the police would find nothing; the Faualos had connections in the police force who warned them beforehand. When off duty, some of the police sneaked in and enjoyed the parties for free. We loved watching the fruitless raids, especially when we watched the cops getting covered with black, stinking mud as they waded through the mosquito-ridden swamps trying to find the bottles.

The police station and main prison in Apia were just across the Vaipe from our home – and connected to us by a large pipe, which we used as a walkway over the stream. Over the years we developed very close relations with the prisoners and police. Every day when the prisoners opened their daily umu, they packed some of the food into a basket and one of them would bring it over the bridge-way to my grandmother. Our mother and grandmother reciprocated by having us deliver food or clothes and other goods to them.

We also sometimes went over and helped the prisoners prepare and cook their daily umu. One of my first published stories, 'The Cross of Soot', is based on that.

After they had served their prison sentences, a couple of male prisoners came and lived with us, and became very loyal members of our aiga.

For entertainment we sometimes sneaked into the courthouse, with the permission of our police friends on duty there, and watched the notorious, sensational cases that took place.

THE TIVOLI

The Tivoli Theatre was the only cinema in Samoa. It was near the main market and just across the stream from our home. Owned by one of the wealthiest families in the country – the Pauls and their Gold Star Company – it was three storeys in height but with two floors inside, and made largely of timber and corrugated iron.

The Tivoli was the most exciting, compulsive, addictive centre of our lives. Hollywood and America seen through the movies were our most powerful foreign influences. The only other public source of information and entertainment was the 2AP, the government-owned and only radio station in Samoa. We listened to that in the mornings before school and at night. But it didn't match the movies in shaping and changing our imaginations and determining how we viewed reality.

The cheapest seats were upstairs and were hard wood; that's where we sat because we couldn't afford the expensive padded seats downstairs.

The first movie I ever saw, I think, was a western with Hopalong Cassidy, who used to be William Boyd. During the smashing, free-for-all bar-room brawl with the baddies, his white Stetson never came off. I fell in love right then with movies. Fortunately our struggling father, who considered the movies a waste of money, gave us enough to go once a week to a matinee.

Sometimes when we didn't have any money, we used to break into the back of the theatre and watch the film through the cracks in the walls. Sometimes we hung round the ticket booth looking sad, and generous people and relatives bought us tickets.

Our older, tougher cousins and their older, tougher Vaipe friends organised a protection racket: for the night sessions, they went through the car park offering to look after cars while their owners attended the sessions. At first people ignored them. But after a few owners came out of the movies to find their cars damaged, they agreed to the 'protection' and tipped our cousins after each session. Needless to say, our cousins had learned about protection rackets from the movies.

Action and adventure, that's what we wanted, so we were intolerant of romances – and sometimes booed during the love scenes. So The Shadow, Flash Gordon, Tom Mix, the Three Stooges, Walt Disney and his menagerie of fabulous creatures, Laurel and Hardy, Roy Rogers and Gene Autry became vital heroes in our lives. We loved the country and western singing! And when Tarzan of the Apes bellowed and beat his mighty chest and swung through the jungle on vines, we were in a high heaven of epic adventure. The Tarzan films were the most popular, and queuing for them sometimes led to riots that the police found difficult to control. Johnny Weissmuller, champion swimmer and vine swinger and bellower, the Tarzan who was in vogue at our time, we mimicked and mimed. 'Me Tarzan, you Jane!' was among the first English phrases we all learned.

The films of Shakespeare's plays were also very popular, despite the fact most of the audience didn't understand much English, let alone Shakespearean English. Why were they popular? I asked myself years later. Ideal Samoan oratory is ornate, poetic, allusory – much like Shakespearean English. Shakespeare's plays are about a strictly hierarchical society, with kings and queens, lords, ladies and commoners. Very much like Samoan society. The most popular play in Samoa was *Romeo and Juliet* – the story of feuding aristocratic families and the fatal love between two of their heirs. Just like feuding Samoan aiga.

So whenever the latest movie of *Romeo and Juliet* hit the Tivoli, the queues erupted, and the audiences wept rivers as they eagerly followed dialogue and plot.

Yes, we learned a lot of English from the movies – American English mainly because most of the movies were American.

Most of the world beyond the reefs – from its geographies, histories, music, languages and conflicts to its dreaming and fantasies – we saw and interpreted through the movies. There was no separation of 'real' and 'unreal'. The outside world was the movies. And we learned more about America and England than about our own country.

In turn we came to see the Vaipe, Apia, Samoa and our lives through those films.

My addiction to films has continued all my life, and has been a crucial influence on my writing and how I view everything.

BOXING

The Tivoli also staged annual national boxing tournaments, which played to loud packed houses. We couldn't afford those so we used to sneak in between our older cousins, who had tickets.

Boxing was a national sport, made popular by the movies that brought us the world championship fights in America and the world. Joe Louis was a Samoan god. To box you need only boxing gloves or bandages to wrap round your fists, so the sport was practised in every village. It was also popularised by the most famous school, the Marist Brothers' School at Mulivai just down the road from us; they taught boxing, and most of Samoa's champions came from there. Our brother Hans was one of their best boxers; he wanted to box in the Tivoli tournaments but our father wouldn't allow him.

At home Uncle Pili and our older cousins taught us boxing even if we didn't want to learn. After the daily lessons we had to box each other, and no crying or giving up was allowed.

Our Uncle Pili was the son of Pepe, my grandmother Mele's sister, and NeeNee, a Chinese medical worker who cared for the Chinese indentured workers. My grandparents adopted Pili as soon as he was born, and raised him according to our grandfather Tuaopepe Tauilo's exacting standards and expectations of what a true male should be.

Pili was only about 1.5 metres tall but he became in my fiction one of the largest characters I've ever created. I based one of my favourite short stories on his life, 'Pint-size Devil on a Thoroughbred'. Pili became a champion jockey and bantamweight boxing champion of Samoa for about four years. Every time he fought in the Tivoli we attended. And because Pili was our uncle, no one dared bully or threaten us with physical violence.

Tauilo, Tuaopepe's nephew from Lefaga, came to stay with us in the Vaipe. He was about 1.9 metres tall with a build as magnificent as Joe Louis's. He aspired to being heavyweight champion, so Pili trained and taught him. It was a strange but marvellous sight, to watch a pint-size devil teaching and training a giant. Pili recruited Tauilo's other sparring partners from our neighbourhood and the marketplace with promises of fame.

In Tauilo's first boxing tournament, he got to the semi-finals by TKO-ing three opponents but lost the finals on a split decision. Pili spent the following week looking for the third judge who, Pili claimed, had been bribed into rigging the split decision. Apparently that judge disappeared into the wilds of Savai'i.

Next boxing season, after nearly a whole year of tough training, Tauilo became heavyweight champion. We were so proud of him, and swaggered round school and Apia as if we were ourselves the champions.

4. IS IT REAL?

Is the Vaipe I've created in my stories, poetry and novels really the Vaipe that existed and exists in real life? Or is it real only in my books? Where does fact end and fiction begin? Is there a difference between the two? And does it matter? Much of the Vaipe in my books no longer exists. I was born into the Vaipe in 1939, and over the seventy-five years since then the Vaipe has changed immensely.

Today, 2015, our God's Little Acre is still there in the centre of the Vaipe, and our Palagi house still stands. The small store is empty and collapsing; my grandmother's and father's graves are always well cared for; the rest of the section has breadfruit, mangoes, bananas and taro on it. Over the years, most of the people who grew up there now live overseas – in New Zealand, Australia and America, with their children and grandchildren.

A few weeks ago I was in Samoa for my brother Joe's funeral. He was the fifth oldest. Seventeen of my other brothers and sisters, numerous cousins, and some of our children and other siblings from overseas and around Samoa were there as well. So we used the occasion to decide what we were going to do with our Vaipe property. Our family home, with a couple looking after it, is now too old to renovate, so we decided that it will be pulled down and replaced with a three-storeyed business building. The land will be raised to stop the flooding, and our father's and grandmother's graves will be raised above flood level and protected.

Joe wanted to be cremated and his ashes placed at our father's feet. So that is where he is now.

MAD ON EDUCATION

Because my family were poor and there were no high schools in Samoa at that time, my father became a plumbing apprentice after he finished primary school.

I have never been able to visualise my father being 'young'. I've always thought of him as immediately becoming a careful, hardworking, frugal adult who saw early that having a good colonial education and learning English, and being thrifty, honest and hardworking, and faithfully pursuing the Christian life were the ways to acquire high status and get out of poverty. With the exception of thrift, his farsighted mother had inculcated those values into him. So they were both mad on us getting a good education – and out-performing, out-competing all the other children in our classes, passing all our exams and acquiring tonnes of certificates and diplomas and degrees that they could hang on our house and fale walls. In her own quiet and loving way, our mother was always there in the background, urging us on and wiping away our disappointed tears when we didn't come top of the class.

Before we went to the primary school at Leifi'ifi, we attended Aoga-a-le-Faifeau. These schools were run by the church pastors or faifeau and held in their houses, the biggest and poshest in the villages. Before secular schools were developed in the early twentieth century, the missionaries established Aoga-a-le-Faifeau to teach reading and writing, and of course the Bible. Within a short time most of our people were literate in Samoan. So I first learned to read in Samoan at our pastor's school and at home.

Our aiga's church is the Ekalesia Fa'alapotopotoga a Iesu i Samoa, the Congregational Church of Jesus in Samoa. It was formed by my pastor Uncle Sanerivi, pastor Pouesi Salamo and Seumanutafa Moepogai, the Ali'i of Apia, who had been prominent in the London Missionary Society Church that dominated Samoa at the time. For reasons I have never been able to find out, a small group of parishioners that included my grandparents and our aiga broke away from the LMS in Apia. From that first congregation has grown our national church. Because of her enormous mana, our grandmother wielded a large influence within that organisation.

When we were children, my father was a lay preacher and influential deacon in our church, and our family, with Uncle Sanerivi and Aunt Ida, started a branch of our church in Malie.

After we started at the secular school, we continued to attend the pastor's school at mid-afternoon during the week. At pastor Pouesi's school, a few kilometres from our home, the discipline was tough and immediate: you sat with your arms folded, cross-legged, and in rows on mats on the hard concrete floor, while Pouesi's wife, Siuila, stood in front with her supple stick. You learned quickly that if you mastered the Samoan alphabet – le Faitau-Pi – well and early and could answer all her questions, you would escape the punishment of her tongue and her stick. As I was often the youngest in my classes, and reticent, respectful and poto (as she kept telling the others), I usually escaped her wrath.

At the pastor's school we learned Samoan (and some English), arithmetic, printing and writing, and whole screeds of the Bible. At the end of every term, strict exams in the three Rs and Bible knowledge were held. Pastors and their wives from our other parishes were the examiners. The exam results were read out publicly.

Most parents turned up to support their children, and wept and chastised them if they didn't do well. And if you came near the bottom of the class, the weeping was angrier and a few children got a walloping that pastor Pouesi had to stop. Even when we came first our father would just say: 'Good but why didn't you get 100 per cent?' Or 'Last time you got 92 percent, why didn't you get more this time?'

By the time I was at the pastor's school, the Wendts were already the ones to beat in the exams. And when we weren't beaten, people would exclaim: 'What do you expect, they're Germans, that's why they're very clever! E ulu Siamagi – they have German heads.' Our grandmother and parents believed that too.

We learned more of the geography and history of the ancient Holy Land than those of our own country.

Nearly all of us Samoans are raised on the Bible, and after over a hundred and fifty years of Christianity (mainly fundamentalist) we know almost nothing of *our* ancient religion. My father's generation knows more about the biblical Holy Land (geographically, historically, spiritually) than our own country, and more about it than the modern Israelis. The biblical prophets, heroes and villains, the courageous saga of the Israelites, Jesus and His disciples, are a vital part of their everyday lives.

For them the Christian Heaven (and Hell), the deserts, plains, rivers and cities of the Holy Land, as depicted in the Bible, are covered eternally with a magic aura – and still exist today. My father *knew* there was a modern Israel but that was not *his* Israel. No, ma'am! His Israel (and its environs, so to speak like my old geography professor) was the one in the Holy Book, which the brave LMS missionaries had transported and replanted in the Darkness of a pagan Samoa to give it Light, a holy Israel which still flourished in the hearts of all *true* Christians. I too was raised on that diet, that Holy Land.

Ola

The pastor had a scroll of colourful biblical pictures; he'd unroll them, one after the other, and get us to read the biblical verses in English under each picture. (God, Jesus and His Disciples were all Papalagi.)

My first sentence in English was: 'And Jesus cried.' I can't remember if my grandmother or the pastor's wife got us to memorise it. But I can still recall it clearly: I am a four-year-old standing alone on the mat, with the late afternoon light pouring over me; I am tight and scared, and want only to disappear into the white illumination. The pastor's wife reaches down, holds the edge of the first scroll and, in one swift upward motion, rolls it over to reveal the next picture. It's a miracle – it's the one I'd prayed for, the beautifully groomed Jesus, luminous robes flowing, hands clasped tightly together, the heavenly light streaming down, and his enormous eyes melting with luminous tears. And even before the pastor's wife points at the English verse under the picture, I am reading it aloud in my grandmother's voice, 'And Jesus cried!' In that moment, the world stands still, applauding, and I am in control of this miracle. I can read the line, the words, for the first time. I can bring sense to those black lines on the page and the scroll. Even more extraordinary – it is in English.

So before I went to secular school, I could read in Samoan, and understand and read some English. Pastor Pouesi and his wife and many of our congregation were proud of the Wendt children excelling in the three Rs and Bible knowledge. Ese le popoko o le fagau a le Au-Wendt! (The children of the Wendts are so bright!)

Eventually my father was appointed pastor of our church in Malie about 11 kilometres out of Apia, so we shifted there. Our grandmother and our other relatives continued living in the Vaipe. Our father continued to work full time at his plumbing business while he was pastor of Malie. So every weekday he drove us to and from Apia to our school and his work.

As a child I didn't know much of our father's earlier history. I knew that he loved music; many of the hymns we sang he'd composed. He taught the piano to my cousin Oata and other young men from the villages, who in turn taught their village church choirs. He met my mother when he was teaching the Vaiala LMS church choir; she had been the lead soprano. I found out that as a young man he'd been able to play any musical instrument in a band, and had trained the Fagali'i village marching band. He'd also formed a dance band with his friends, the Rasmussen brothers, and had been band leader and pianist. On Sunday evenings after lotu, he always listened to the BBC classical music hour on the 2AP.

Our father had a remarkable capacity for work. When he finished his plumbing apprenticeship, he worked for Bryan Williams's grandfather for a couple of years and then started his own business. He rented a small room in Saleufi and, with his plumbing tools in a sack, walked to fix people's plumbing. Later, he bought a bicycle for work, and, near the end of our primary schooling, an old Ford car and converted it into a truck we called 'Bob'. By that time his cousin Ron NeeNee and brother Rudy and nephew Snooky and other relatives were working for him. The business was now in larger premises and even had a telephone.

Our father never bought anything until he could pay cash for it. So the expansion of his business and everything he owned was always debt free. We advised him years later to borrow a large amount of money from his bank to buy the Catholic land in Saleufi that he was then leasing for his business. He didn't say anything, refusing to buy the land on credit. Two years later he bought it – with money he'd saved.

After a hard day's work he would bring home a few beers, and get some of us to open the bottles and serve him his drinks. Some Friday evenings he would invite over Faualo's son, Fuli, and they would drink until they were talking loudly and then singing. Our older relatives told us that our father used to drink and party a lot during his dance band days.

As he became more successful in business, he relinquished his gift for music. I never saw him play the piano. Not long after he became a deacon, he stopped drinking altogether and preached against it from the pulpit.

THE SECULAR SCHOOL

The secular education system was truly colonial. The village government schools were for Samoans and were in Samoan; Europeans were excluded, especially half-castes or afakasi, who were classified as European. The only English-language primary school, Leifi'ifi, was reserved for the children of Europeans and the administrators. So, as afakasi, we were able to attend that school. I've used that experience in much of my fiction.

Monroe was my mother's maiden name. (Her father's father was an American.) My father's surname is Lagona, an ali'i in Sapepe, our village on the western tip of Upolu.

Leifi'ifi School was considered the best primary school, but it was reserved, by the colonial administration, for Papalagi and Afakasi children. So, to get me into that exclusive school, my astute father registered me under my mother's maiden name. I wasn't aware of that until two weeks before starting school, when my father explained he wanted me to use my mother's surname so we would remember her always. 'Apart from that,' he continued, 'I want you to have the best education possible. Your mother's name will get you into Leifi'ifi, where all the brightest children go.'

'What's my new name?' I asked.

'It's an American name,' he said. 'Monroe.' Because I knew no English, it sounded like a drawn-out grunt. 'Monroe,' my father repeated slowly. 'M-O-N-R-O-E,' he spelled it. And with that, I heard it for the first time.

'Monroe!' I sang, clapping my hands.

'Yes, that's correct. You're very bright.'

That day I skipped everywhere, singing to myself, 'Monroe, Monroe, Monroe.' I varied the pronunciation and tune, rolling the syllables, like hard round sweets, around my mouth.

Next day when three of my friends came to play, I told them proudly, 'I have an American name!'

'What?' Ianeta said.

'Yes, I have my mother's American name!' They gazed at me. 'Monroe,' I revealed. 'That's my name.'

'Liar,' Ianeta whispered, without malice. (They just didn't believe me, that was all.)

'It's true,' I insisted. 'My father told me yesterday.' They refused to believe me. 'I can spell it in English!' I boasted.

'Spell it then,' Ianeta demanded. (Ianeta wasn't my favourite friend.)

I concentrated hard, my eyes shut tightly. Then I spelled it. I opened my eyes to their sighs of envy. 'Monroe was my mother's grandfather, who came from America a long time ago,' I pressed home my attack.

'So you're an Afakasi!' Malia, my most perceptive friend, remarked. I nodded, but before I could boast more about my American ancestry, they skipped off to play under the shady gatae trees behind our house. I followed them.

For a while as we played hopscotch, they succeeded in not voicing their envy. But eventually, Salome, the youngest, couldn't hold it back any longer.

'But you can't speak English!' she said.

'So how can you go to Leifi'ifi?' Ianeta attacked.

'The Palagi teachers will find out and send you back home!' Malie snared me further.

I was trapped. 'I ... I *can* speak a little English.'

'Say something in English then!' Salome challenged me.

'You're just jealous!' I changed tactics.

'I'm not!' said Salome.

'I'm not!' chorused Malia.

'And I'm not!' echoed Ianeta.

I was hooked by their accusing silence. 'You are!' I snapped, miserable because they *were* telling the truth. I started walking back to our house.

'MA-NI-ROU!' Ianeta chanted, parodying me. The others echoed her.

I fled home as fast as I could.

So until I was married (for the first time) years later, Monroe was my surname.

Ola

One day during my third year at Leifi'ifi primary school, our Papalagi teacher (Miss Bristol, who we all loved) told us during a social studies lesson that Jacob Roggeveen, a Dutch explorer, had discovered Samoa in 1722. My imagination immediately conjured forth a vision of his magnificent masted ship breaking through the horizon in a blaze of sun and cloud. I considered this a radical addition to my understanding of our country, knowledge that made me look afresh at everything. And I wanted our grandmother, Mele – at that time the most influential person in my life – to know about it. So I rushed home after school and asked her:

'Did you know that a Dutch man by the name of Jacob Roggeveen discovered our country?'

Patiently, she asked, 'Who told you that?'

'Our teacher,' I proudly divulged.

'Were we Samoans here before the Papalagi came?' she replied, slow smile on her face.

'Yes.'

'Was this man Roggeveen a Papalagi?' Her scrutiny was now focused on my face fully, patiently, expectantly. 'Where do Dutch people come from?' She helped me.

'Holland,' I replied, with the truth of the matter sliding into my vision and occupying it. 'So he was a Papalagi,' I admitted.

'So when you go to school tomorrow, tell your teacher that *we* discovered our country. Tell her we've been here for at least 3,000 years,' she said.

Now I was on fire with pride in my ancestors' achievements, prouder than I'd been about Roggeveen.

I was very fortunate to have had that lesson about decolonising ourselves when I was so young.

That set me off on a journey that continues today: of challenging colonial perceptions of us, our histories and our ways of life; of trying to understand how our ancestors viewed themselves, their environment and the cosmos; of trying to comprehend what has happened to us in our intermingling and fusing over the last few centuries. Much of my writing has been about that.

5. INTO A WORLD OF BOOKS

At Leifi'ifi primary school we were taught in English, so we had to learn English (both spoken and written) quickly in order to survive. Speaking Samoan was forbidden. I could read and write in Samoan from the pastor's school and my father's and grandmother's teaching at home. I could also read some English. We didn't have many books in our home, but we grew up in a culture rich in oral traditions, especially those drawn from the Bible and told by our grandmother, as I've described.

I loved the world of books that I now found myself in, and became addicted to reading the written word and the English language: school journals, illustrated children's books, science books, nature books, maths books and anything else I could find.

While growing up in the Vaipe and going to primary school, did I ever want to write my own stories, be a writer? I don't think that ever came into my mind. I just wanted to enjoy school, learning and absorbing everything. I was painfully self-conscious, and though I loved hearing and reading stories, I was rarely able to get up and tell any. In our English classes we had to write stories, often just a couple of paragraphs, about topics such as 'On my way to school this morning', or 'What I did during the school holidays'. And then read them to our class. But I never thought that one day I'd be a writer. The writers of the books we were reading were not Samoan; they were all Europeans living in a fabulous beyond-the-reefs world. And none of the characters in their illustrated books looked like us.

During our schooling we were all influenced, touched, inspired and changed by certain teachers who we will remember for the rest of our lives.

In my first years at Leifi'ifi, our teacher was Miss Bristol, a New Zealander in her thirties. She was always beautifully dressed, and she spoke slowly and clearly so that we could all understand her. She was the palest person we had ever seen and her skin glowed, giving her a magical aura that made us believe she possessed great spiritual powers. And when she sat on her low chair and gathered us, sitting cross-legged on the mats, around her – and then opened a storybook and started to read from it – that power captivated us instantly. Like my grandmother, she had the mana of a gifted storyteller. And I fell in love with her and her stories, which in turn reinforced my love of books, the English language and learning.

In Standard One our teacher was Mrs Mary Brebner. She had ebony skin and was beautiful, with flowing black hair and a sculptured face with high cheek bones. She was strict but forgiving when we made errors. She was a patient, gifted teacher who made me understand our school lessons easily, and inspired us to learn more. Some of us cried at the end of her year with us.

Throughout primary school, her son Charlie and I were in the same classes and he was one of my best friends. He used to bring large lunches to school, which he shared with us. One day after school he took us to his house, and shared some soursop fruit (they had a small orchard of them) and iced water. It was the first time I'd ever tasted iced water or ice cubes – they were shockingly cold on my hands and even more shocking as the ice slid down my astounded throat. I'd not known such cold before.

Later in life I found out from Mrs Brebner's daughters that their mother always followed my career with pride, telling everyone that she'd once taught me.

She lived into her nineties and at least three generations of Samoans are indebted to her for their education. I autographed one of my novels (I think it was *Leaves of the Banyan Tree*) with a thank you note for her, and one of her daughters gave it to her. Apparently she showed the book to everyone who visited her.

Mr Robert (Bob) Rankin was a New Zealander who'd been in the Armed Forces, stationed as an intelligence officer in Japan at the end of the Second World War. He always wore immaculate white shirts and shorts, long white socks and black shoes to school. He was fluent in Japanese, which he would sometimes break into during his teaching. Most astounding was his ability to chew and eat chalk as he paced the classroom. He so clearly loved literature and reading and teaching, and he inspired us to learn more.

The Forsgrens, one of Apia's prominent families, owned a photographic business not far from the Vaipe. Bob Rankin courted and married the oldest Forsgren daughter. And when he quit teaching he started a newspaper, the *Samoana*, which became a powerful influence on our country's politics. He was one of the Government's main critics.

Bob and his wife established a lucrative printmaking business in Vaoala. Ancient Samoan siapo and tatau designs that they researched became the hallmark of the hand-printed fabrics that became famous throughout the Pacific and the wider world. He had huge energy and drive, and was always ready to pursue new ideas and try out new ventures.

When I returned and taught at Samoa College in the 1960s I taught the Rankin children, who were exceptionally bright, dedicated and hard-working.

I edited the rival newspaper, the *Bulletin*, and disagreed often and publicly with Bob about politics and other issues. We became and remained friends.

Mr Leta'a Sulu Devoe taught us in Standard Four, I think. He was very handsome, and well known in Samoa as a pianist and choirmaster. Mr Devoe was also our organist and choirmaster at the Apia Protestant Church. As a teacher he was thorough, always extremely well prepared, and taught maths and science, in particular, with flair, commitment and knowledge.

He later became Director-in-Charge of the first fire station in Apia. When I returned to teach at Samoa College, he still played the organ at our church, and we became good friends. When he died, I attended his funeral service at Alamagoto, his home church, and presented his wife with a copy of *Leaves of the Banyan Tree*, with a message in it farewelling him and telling him how much I owed him.

SCHOLARSHIPPER

In Form One at Apia Intermediate School, our teacher was the first Samoan to graduate from a New Zealand teachers' training college. Epi Enari was the daughter of one of the most famous LMS pastors, and we all looked forward to being in her class.

She was strict, hard-working and demanding. She kept inspiring us to win scholarships to go to New Zealand and qualify as doctors and lawyers – the most desirable occupations in the eyes of all Samoans. The scholarship scheme, which the New Zealand administration had established, was only a few years old; and was aimed at selecting young Samoans to be educated in New Zealand then to return and work in the civil service and the professions.

These scholarships were the most prestigious and sought-after educational awards in the country; every parent, aiga, church, village wanted them. The scholarships were very generous, paying for all your travel, clothing and schooling and other expenses at boarding school, and an end-of-the-year holiday in Samoa with your aiga every three years. And if you graduated well from high school, the scholarship paid for you to study at university or training college or another tertiary institution. Winning one also brought huge publicity, honour and status. Until Samoa College, the first high school in Samoa, was opened in 1953, only the few wealthy families, mainly afakasi and Palagi, could afford to send their children to boarding schools in New Zealand. These scholarships were the only opportunity for families like mine.

To get a scholarship you had to sit a national exam, which only students who were below fifteen years old and in Form One or Form Two could sit. I was one of a few in our Form One who was eligible. My brother Felix, in Form Two, was also eligible. I can't recall how many students sat the exam, but I remember that about three classrooms at our school were filled with exam candidates. I think the exam – which lasted about two hours – was a mix of English comprehension, arithmetic, general knowledge and social studies.

Before the exam our teacher, Epi Enari, made a few of us stay behind after school for special coaching. When Felix and I got home after that, we were expected to shower and eat; then after evening lotu, during which our father prayed loudly and poetically for our success in the exam, we had to settle down in our mosquito net and revise and revise and revise. If we went to the pastor's school, pastor Pouesi took us aside and taught us what he considered to be the 'arithmetic' in the scholarship exam. Then, with all the other children present, he prayed fervently for our success. In church on Sunday, the preachers made special mention of us and beseeched 'the Almighty God of all Knowledge to grant us a pass in this devilishly difficult exam'.

Instead of making me feel confident about my chances, all this heightened teacher, family, church and community support and expectation induced huge fears of failure in me. I was going to disappoint so many people!

At that time, I looked up particularly to my two oldest brothers, Hans and Felix. When I was still unable to swim, Hans and Felix and other older siblings took us swimming at the pool into which the Vaipe flowed behind the Mulivai Cathedral. Those of us who couldn't swim were instructed by Hans not to go into the water – we were to play on the banks.

Hans and the other older ones were yelling and screaming as they played chasey in the pool and across it. Watching them excited me so much that I edged across the mud bank and more and more into the water. Before I realised it, I was swallowing the choking water and my desperate feet were trying to grip onto the bottom of the pool. I flailed and started screaming. Suddenly there was a wild flurry of someone gripping my hair and dragging me out of the water, gasping for air, gasping for life. Hans!

On our way home he told us not to tell our parents. (We hadn't asked for permission to go swimming.) He put his arm around me and told me to stop crying. He'd saved me for today. I've always been grateful to him.

Felix usually topped his classes – he worked so hard to do that – and was very good at sports, especially running.

And when Hans and Felix sensed I was suffering

great stress preparing for the exam, they both sat with me and soothed my fears by telling me how proud they were of me and how well I was doing at school. The exam would be easy for me.

But once the exam came, the stress didn't interfere. I settled into the exam paper, realising with mounting confidence that I could cope with it. Time slowed down. I didn't panic when a few students finished early and strode up to the exam supervisors with their scripts. I steadied myself and followed Ms Enari's advice that we should use all the allocated time and recheck and recheck what we had written.

Felix sat the exam with the other Form Two candidates in the next classroom, so I didn't see him until it was over.

The exam scripts were marked in New Zealand. I can't remember when we first heard the results. I think our headmaster first informed my parents and Ms Enari, and then announced them to our whole school. The scholarships became the main national news over 2AP that night and for the next few days.

My family's joy, euphoria and pride at my winning a scholarship had a ragged sad hole in it. Felix missed out. Why? There were only seven scholarships that year. Felix and I had both passed the exam, so there were two Wendts in the selection. They chose me because I was younger and closer to the age of Form Two students in New Zealand. This is what, I recall, they told our headmaster, who then told our father.

To console Felix and our upset mother and aiga, our father said we needn't worry about Felix because he had an unbreakable will to succeed in anything he chose.

Our father was absolutely correct about my brother. Felix was dux of Apia Intermediate that year, and dux later at Samoa College, passing School Certificate and winning a scholarship to study at Wellington College in New Zealand. He attended Massey University, graduated, returned to Samoa with his wife Marita, and taught for a while; then he won a scholarship to the University of Hawai'i, where he graduated with a Master's in agricultural science, and went on to Cornell University and got a PhD. Felix was the first Samoan to be a professor of agriculture, and for many years was the Head of the School of Agriculture at the University of the South Pacific. Later he was appointed Samoa's ambassador to the United States and the United Nations.

From the day the country and our aiga heard we were the scholarship winners, everyone treated us in a special way. Everywhere I went, I felt I was being watched and commented upon, envied and treated with extra generosity and respect. It made me even shyer and more inward-looking and reticent.

During the stretch of my life as a 'scholarshipper', every time we returned from New Zealand for the school holidays, I had to survive that extra scrutiny: everywhere we were seen as people with a special future, a future of helping our country. Within my own aiga, my parents and Mele and other elders held me up to our other young people as the model to follow.

Being awarded that scholarship changed my life for ever. And when Felix and many of my other brothers and sisters later won the same scholarships and were educated in New Zealand, Australia and the United States, this transformed the life of our aiga. These scholarships and study abroad turned the Wendt family into the large, complex, multilingual, multi-ethnic international aiga it is today.

6. BECOMING A NEW ZEALAND PROTECTED PERSON

I was thirteen years old. I had never been outside Samoa, never been on a ship, never experienced winter or snow, never worn a tie or a long-sleeved shirt or a suit or socks, and put shoes on only once. I didn't know how to eat with a knife and fork or dress myself the Palagi way. Most of what I knew about New Zealand came from the movies and books and teachers – and my grandmother, who had lived in New Zealand in the 1920s.

My grandmother had gone with the Palagi family she was working for in Samoa to visit that family's family in Cambridge, a small farming town in the Waikato. She cared for the family's children. When she told us, year after year, about that visit, her stories assumed the dizzying quality of myth. Trains were Nofoa-afi, thrones-of-fire – a series of long houses attached together in one long line and pulled by an engine of fire. They bellowed like whales, and clanged and clinged, and went chugga-chugga-chugga along glistening iron rails that stretched on forever.

All Papalagi people wore false teeth, she told us. Because of their bad diet they had bad teeth, which had to be pulled out early in their lives. Papalagi restricted their families to just the husband and wife and two children – it was cheaper that way, and they didn't like wasting their money on fa'alavelave.

Māori, the tagata moni, true people, of New Zealand, were suffering terrible dispossession by the Papalagi settlers, she maintained. But they, like us Samoans, were fighting valiantly against that.

The scholarshippers were brought together to prepare for our shift to New Zealand. The other six were Viopapa Annandale, Karanita Enari, Pito Fa'alogo, Iulai Toma, Vaeluaga Reti and Salome Neru. Karanita Enari was Epi Enari's adopted son. Apart from that, I didn't know anything about them.

Arrangements were in the hands of an Education Department officer, the older brother of one of my best friends, Clement Meredith. The seven of us met at the Education Department to fill in forms, and at the hospital for our medical tests, then at the immigration office to fix our travel papers. Apart from Viopapa, who had done some overseas travelling, we found the process bewildering, but we were guided through it with patience, care and humour. Some of our parents also accompanied us.

At the end of it all, we each received an official immigration document entitled 'New Zealand Protected Person', with our photographs in the top right-hand corner and all the information about us and our right to enter and stay in New Zealand. I was a New Zealand Protected Person.

And by the end of this process, all of us boys were friends. So were the girls. We sensed that we needed to stick together, helping one another survive the threatening unknown that confronted us.

In those days you couldn't buy ready-made suits or long-sleeved shirts and other winter clothes in the Apia shops. So my Aunt Ida, a skilled seamstress, got a large man's thick green woollen suit from somewhere and picked it apart. I had to suffer the material's rough, prickly feel while she measured me for the suit. It was double-breasted and heavy and hot. Needless to say, while I was being outfitted in front of my whole aiga, I was encouraged and praised by the adults but some of the young ones quietly sniggered. At one point I cried, and my mother chased them away. I withdrew deeper into my cocoon of self-consciousness. The clothes for New Zealand felt so alien, and I was convinced I looked stupid in them.

As I was being outfitted, my grandmother and Aunt Ida were teaching me how to sit at a Papalagi dining table, use the cutlery and crockery, eat in silence and slowly with my mouth closed, and still be able to carry a polite conversation.

VOYAGING INTO THE COLD

Ships had to dock out in the middle of Apia Harbour and use lighters to load and unload. The two main ships that served the New Zealand–Pacific Islands route were the *Matua* and the *Tofua*, owned by the Union Steamship Company. The ships transported goods and produce, such as copra and bananas, and people.

We were to travel on the *Matua*, and the journey would take a week, with a stop of two days in Suva, Fiji. I'd not been on a long sea trip or a ship like that before, and thinking about what could happen only added to my sense of almost overwhelming dread.

At school a cloak of sadness was winding itself around me and my friends; we knew we were separating but we didn't want it to happen. Not yet. Even Ms Enari treated me with great gentleness, afraid we might break down in tears.

It was all weighing heavily. A few nights before leaving, I must have suffered nightmares and woke screaming. My mother held me tightly for the first time that I can recall. Tightly as if she wasn't ever going to let me go. She held me until I fell asleep – and for the rest of my life I will never forget her consoling warmth and her scent of coconut oil and alofa.

The evening before I left, my family held a farewell lotu and dinner. Reverend Pouesi and Mrs Pouesi and other deacons, a couple of my friends, my Uncle Tunupopo and Aunt Fiapa'ipa'i and a few of my Vaiala aiga came, and some of our neighbours. The rest were my Wendt aiga.

I sat beside my father near Reverend Pouesi, and felt utterly conspicuous. Led by Mrs Pouesi, everyone sang a couple of fervent family hymns. One of the deacons read at length from the Bible, then the Reverend Pouesi preached a short sermon about God blessing those who are intelligent and hard-working and loyal to God, like me, and then wished me well on my journey into that 'cold, foreign and godless country called New Zealand'.

Then the huge, huge feast that my mother and grandmother and aiga had prepared was served.

For the first time in my life, I was served my own food mat. I wasn't hungry – I was too tight with sadness, fear and regret. And my brothers and sisters were not allowed to sit with me. My mother came over and, sitting down beside me, her warm knee pressing up against mine, started breaking up our taro and putting pieces on my plate. I glanced up at her. Smiling softly, her eyes aglow with alofa for me, she whispered, 'Don't worry, everything will be all right.'

Then the next day it was early evening, with the setting sun spilling a layer of golden light across the harbour and the ship as I said goodbye to my friends and my aiga on the crowded jetty. I cried freely, especially when I farewelled Hans and Felix. My father steered me down into the lighter; my mother and grandmother and a few other aiga followed.

A strong breeze buffeted us as the lighter headed for the ship. The lighter was full of the other scholarshippers and their families. The layers of floral ula that my aiga had wound round my neck came up to my ears, and I could barely see over them. I began to wheeze because of the strong smell of the flowers. I took one ula off and put it round my mother's neck, another for my grandmother, and some for my aunts, until I had only two round my neck.

We clambered up the precarious gangway onto the main deck and into the acrid smell of diesel. It was a smell that triggered my nausea repeatedly throughout the voyage.

The four boys shared a cabin two decks below with two double bunks. The purser led us and our families down to our cabin through the crowded corridors and the increasing heat and diesel smell.

We all made a quick inspection of our cabin: strange, new. My mother packed away my clothes in the lockers. We went back up to the top deck and the refreshing breeze. It was crowded with other families and passengers exploring the deck and looking back at the shore and the crowd of people waving there. We did the same, avoiding the soon inevitable fact of farewell. It was darkening; the sun was now over the horizon.

I avoided looking at my mother, and she at me.

Then over the loudspeaker: 'All non-passengers must now go to the lighters. We will be sailing soon.'

And the weeping began again, first quietly as we embraced and kissed and moved towards the gangway, then more loudly. My parents were the last to go down the gangway, my mother stopping often, wiping her eyes and turning and waving to me.

As the jetty and shoreline and outline of Upolu disappeared into the darkness, we stood at the railing waving.

We went down to our cabin, realising for the first time we were now on our own. We draped all our ula around the opened cabin portholes and put our suitcases away. Then someone said it was dinner time, so we hurried up to the bar and dining-room, steadying ourselves against the rolling of the ship.

I felt utterly exposed when we entered the brightly lit dining room and I saw that most of the tables were occupied. The white tablecloths, cutlery and crockery glittered. The girls were already seated at a table with what looked like a Palagi family. We waved to them as our waiter took us to our table where a Polynesian man and his grown-up son were seated.

The two men rose to their feet, greeting us. He was a doctor from Tonga, and he was taking his son to medical school in New Zealand. 'I understand you're all students going to boarding school,' he said, smiling. 'I went to boarding school in New Zealand too,' he added. 'But that was a long time ago.'

'I went to my father's old school,' his son said. 'Auckland Boys' Grammar.'

Once we were seated, and we'd introduced ourselves to him, he said, 'I know you're all from Christian families, so I'll say grace.' I felt, with rising gratitude and relief, that he was going to look after us, show us how to cope with the ship and everything and everyone in it.

When the waiter came to take our orders, he showed us how to use the menu, telling us what he was ordering and suggesting what we could have, starting with soup, then the mains, then the dessert.

When our food arrived, we copied how they used the cutlery, and which order they followed. He kept nodding whenever we got it right.

I woke in the middle of the night and my stomach and head were rolling with the ship. I tried to ignore it but couldn't. Karanita, who was in the bunk under mine, stirred, got out of bed and headed for the door. I followed him, and we clambered up to the open deck into the cool hands of the light spray that splashed cold sea over our faces, distracting us from the nausea.

When we went back down, Pito and Iulai, who were not seasick, suggested we have cold showers to rid ourselves of the dizziness. We did, and it worked.

However, at breakfast with the ship rocking and rolling more, Karanita and I only managed to finish the porridge, which the doctor suggested we have, and then had to rush back to our cabins and our beds, where we lay clutching at the sides of the bunks.

A short while later I was vomiting into the toilet bowl. Karanita had to do the same.

During the voyage, Iulai and Pito never suffered severe seasickness, if I'm remembering accurately. And they looked after us. Karanita got his sea legs after almost two days. The Tongan doctor came on the second day that I was absent from breakfast and examined me, restricting my diet to oranges, plain tea, fruit drinks and water, and some toast.

Iulai, Pito and Karanita took turns bringing me my meals, which I never finished. Some of the girls were also suffering seasickness, so the boys also took meals to them.

During the day they also periodically checked on how I was. All this strengthened our friendship.

The ocean and the rocking and rolling and diesel smell seemed endless.

But on the third morning I felt steady enough to go to breakfast as the ship entered Suva Harbour and its still, waveless water.

When the ship docked, the other boys helped me and the girls onto the wharf to meet the Samoan pastor and his Fijian wife who were waiting for us. Once on land, I could control the swaying in the ground under me – and in my stomach.

The pastor and his wife put me to sleep in their sitting room on a sofa while they showed the others round town. It was healing and consoling not being able to smell the diesel and feel the ship plunging into the troughs.

But in the remaining four days of our voyage, the sea got rougher, the air colder and greyer.

ARRIVAL AND DISPERSAL

A first cousin of my father's, Ron NeeNee, trained under and worked for my father as a plumber. In the late 1940s he migrated to Auckland with his wife Moka. My cousin Ida went to Auckland in 1950 and stayed with them as she worked as a typist. My father notified them I was coming.

So Ida and Moka and a Palagi scholarship officer were waiting for us on the Auckland wharf. The wharf and earth continued to sway under me like the ocean and would do so for weeks, and nausea loomed all too often. I'd known Ida well when I stayed with my relatives in Malie; she was always gentle, kind and considerate. So I was comforted to see her and Moka.

They took us in taxis to stay at the YMCA before

we dispersed to our schools. Auckland was the noisiest place I'd ever been in; all around us, as we drove through the heavy traffic and high buildings and down-pressing grey sky, I felt a mixture of intimidation, awe and a wish not to be there.

The YMCA building and bunk-bed room were the largest I'd ever slept in. But the room became claustrophobic as the ocean continued to move. At breakfast that morning, I ate a strange breakfast of fried liver and bacon and toast. But then nausea erupted. I ran from the table but started spewing across the dining room. I was so ashamed. Pito and Karanita cleaned up my vomit and Iulai took me back to our room.

Ida came and took me to stay with the NeeNees at Wellington Street, Freeman's Bay, for a day and night. Moka and Ron had five children and a nephew, all younger than me. They were very open, welcoming and generous, showing me their games, books and toys, and telling me about their schools. But because they reminded me so much of my sisters and brothers, they increased my homesickness.

Two days later another Palagi scholarship officer, a blond and bespectacled middle-aged man from Pacific Island Affairs, came and collected me from the YMCA.

The day before that I'd tearfully farewelled the other six scholarshippers. Pito and Iulai were off to

Scots College in Wellington, Viopapa to St Mary's College in Stratford, Karanita to Timaru Boys' High School, Salome Neru to New Plymouth Girls' High School, and I can't recall where Vaeluaga Reti went to. So I was feeling profoundly alone, and my longing to be back home with my mother and family was like an unclenching fist in my belly. I wept when I said goodbye to Ida, who promised I was coming to stay with her for the school holidays.

I'd not been on a train before, but my grandmother (and the movies) had given me some knowledge of them. But it was a long, loudly chugging, periodically screeching night. The engine's smoke sometimes invaded our carriage and the acrid smell and feel of black coal smoke tainted everything. It felt as if we were hurtling into the mouth of a dangerous animal. Our carriage was full, so I had to try to sleep sitting up, next to the scholarship officer – and for a while I couldn't.

But I woke when the train stopped at a station. People scrambled out and bought food and hot tea and other drinks. My travelling guide got us a meat pie and a mug of tea each. I forced myself to eat the pie – and liked it. The tea I found too strong.

The rest of the night was a series of those stops for refreshments and my inability to sleep.

Palagi toilets – and train toilets in this case – were still foreign and threatening so I tried to hold it all in. But by early dawn I couldn't hold it anymore and I rushed to the toilet, worked up the courage to open it and entered. There I spewed loudly and in large streams into the bowl. Kneeling, I held onto the bowl and continued until I was throwing up only bile. By now I was feeling free of the nausea.

We got off in Whanganui early in the morning and had to wait for the bus to New Plymouth. At breakfast in a small restaurant, I could only eat two bites of a piece of toast and swallow a bit of tea. I felt as if everyone was staring at me. I thought they were being critical of how I was dressed (in my thick green suit and green tie) and my obvious ignorance of their way of life. For the first time I was blatantly aware I was the only brown person there – and everywhere. My dizziness returned.

Concerned about my state, the scholarship officer got us seated just behind the bus driver so I would have a clear view of the road ahead. And he told me to concentrate on that view to stop my car sickness. And on that miserable bus trip, with bright skies and the lush landscape of dairy farms spreading neatly up to the mountain range on our left, that was all I concentrated on.

TARANAKI

Then I saw the Mountain – a white-topped symmetrical cone, which my travelling companion said was Mt Egmont. And as we moved along, the Mountain watched me, steadying my homesickness.

I'd not seen anything like that before, towering and inescapable as it dominated the landscape with its welcoming, all-encompassing presence. That Mountain – which I later preferred to call by its indigenous name, Taranaki – was to be present in my vision during my whole life at boarding school (and later) as a healing, wise, consoling elder like my grandmother. Taranaki has remained one of my ancestral mountains to this day.

… Taranaki Who witnessed Te Whiti's fearless stand at Parihaka

against the settlers' avaricious laws and guns

Who watched them being evicted and driven eventually

from their lands but not from the defiant struggle

their descendants continue today forever until victory

'The Ko'olau', in *From Mānoa to a Ponsonby Garden*

NIGER HOUSE

We arrived at Niger House, where all the Prep School students boarded, a few days before school started for the year. As the taxi drove up the concrete driveway with the double-storeyed wooden building with wide verandas and fire escapes looming up ahead, I anticipated the departure of my travelling companion who had made me feel safe – and my feeling of abandonment clogged my senses again.

We got out of the taxi. My companion told the driver to wait. He picked up my large suitcase and, looking kindly at me and seeing that I was on the verge of tears, said: 'We're here. I know you're missing your parents and family. Be brave and you'll be okay.' He put his arm round my shoulders and guided me to the front veranda.

The high front double door was open. No one in sight.

He pressed the door bell and the ringing echoed loudly through the cavernous house. A door on the left along the corridor opened and a man with black-rimmed glasses, short-cropped wavy black hair and rosy cheeks hurried up towards us, smiling.

'I'm Alan Gardiner,' he introduced himself to my companion, who shook hands with him. 'And this must be Albert Wendt,' he added, smiling more broadly, reaching down and shaking my hand. 'Welcome to Niger House, your new home.'

I tried to smile, I tried to loosen the feeling of abandonment, I tried to swallow the tears that were now in my throat.

'Albert is a long way from home,' the scholarship officer said, 'and I know he is feeling very homesick.'

'I think I understand,' said Mr Gardiner. 'We've had other Island boys in our house before. We'll do our best to make him feel at home here.' He reached over and my companion handed him my suitcase. He turned and waved us past. The scholarship officer stepped into the house and I followed. 'None of the other boys are here yet – most of them will be here on Sunday and Monday,' Mr Gardiner said.

Mr Gardiner led us up the corridor to the foot of the impressive staircase that led upstairs. We stopped there and my companion said, 'Albert, I'm leaving you here – I have to catch the train back.' His face was suffused with concern. He gripped my shoulder, turned and hurried out of the front door.

Mr Gardiner took me upstairs to the middle dormitory, a circular room with high ceilings, six beds with bedside tables and a highly polished wooden floor. 'Seeing you're the first here, you can choose which bed you want,' he offered, smiling. I chose the middle one against and under the large front windows. This was the first bed that was to be mine alone. He laid my suitcase on my bed. 'Later you can put your clothes into that.' He pointed at the dressing table near the head of my bed. 'Now I'll show you the rest of your home.'

As we moved round the two storeys, through the other dormitories, the locker rooms, the toilets and shower block, I felt intimidated by all the newness. All I wanted was to be safely back in Samoa. Mr Gardiner must have sensed that and invited me to meet his wife. 'You must be really tired, so we'll just have a cold drink with Mrs Gardiner and then you can go up and have a sleep.'

The Gardiners' large apartment was attached to the northern side of the house. I didn't really want to meet or be with other strangers, but he held my arm and led me gently into their sitting room.

Out of the dining room a slim woman, about her husband's height, with light blond hair, a finely chiselled face, a beaming smile and quick enthusiastic movements stepped out and hurried to me. 'Hello, Albert,' she greeted me, almost kneeling, and reaching over and clasping my reluctant hand. 'We want you to treat this as your home,' she whispered. 'We know you're a long, long way from home. Come.' She guided me to the large dining table on which there was a tray of glasses and a jug full of a cloudy liquid. Mr Gardiner pulled out the nearest chair and I sat down while she poured me a drink. 'This is made from our own lemons,' she said. Mr Gardiner sat down beside me.

I sat trying not to look at my drink or at them. 'Cheers,' Mr Gardiner said. I didn't understand, so he raised his glass and took a drink. I copied him. So did Mrs Gardiner.

The cool tart/sweet taste thawed my mouth and gullet and belly. Slowly it relieved some of my nausea, shyness and refusal to be part of that family and that house.

As I left to go upstairs to rest, Mr Gardiner handed me a thick blue dressing gown. 'Here, I'm sure you're cold, so use that.'

'And you have a good rest,' she said.

I slept fitfully – I couldn't get my feet completely warm and this would be a problem for me for the next two or so years. Then I must have suffered some fearful dreams and woke crying. Mr Gardiner came rushing into my dormitory and, making me sit up, got me to wear the dressing gown then guided me down into their apartment, into their warm sitting room where a fire was now burning.

'I think he's been having nightmares,' he said to his wife.

'We know its summer but being from the Islands you must be cold,' Mrs Gardiner said to me, softly. 'So I've put a fire on.' She reached over and wrapped the collar of the dressing gown more tightly round my neck. 'And you can sleep here.' She indicated the long sofa opposite the fireplace, which she'd turned into a bed.

I must have been whimpering audibly because she sat me down on the sofa, settled beside me and held my hands. 'It's all right, Albert, we know you must be really missing your parents. So if you want to cry, go ahead.'

And I did.

After I had dried my eyes and had a hot cup of cocoa, she told me to lie down and try to go to sleep. They switched off the lights.

A short while later I was afloat in a calm, healing ocean of sleep, which I didn't want to swim out of.

And when I woke the next morning it was to the alofa, generosity and endless caring of the Gardiners: Christine and Alan Gardiner and their baby daughter Robyn, a relationship that I have treasured to this day.

The classes for the whole school for 1953 were to start the following Tuesday, and all the boarders were supposed to check in over the weekend, starting on the Saturday afternoon, through Sunday and into Monday. So I was the only student in our house until Sunday evening.

In that time I took all my meals with the Gardiners and, when homesickness threatened severely, I slept in their sitting room in front of the fire.

Nearly every morning when I woke, I heard a tenor voice coming from their apartment. Sometimes the well-controlled voice sang a song that at the time I found strange but I would later come to know as opera. I learned over the next few months that Mr Gardiner was a well-known tenor who played leading roles in the productions – mainly Gilbert and Sullivan operas – of the local operatic society.

On Saturday morning Mr Gardiner took me up to the main school and showed me round the expansive grounds, gym and swimming pool, and buildings. He took particular care to show me the main school assembly hall. As we moved round it, he paused at the photographs that had Pasefika students in them and told me their names and what they had achieved. Some of them were still there in their final year. Most had been prefects, and 1st XV and 1st XI players, and most had gone on to be in the professions. I felt encouraged by their success.

I was always aware the Mountain was watching us.

Then when we were in the Prep School building, he let me pick out the desk I wanted. He also gave me detailed information about the Prep School, which was closing down at the end of that year. Only a Form Two class, of thirty students, was left. He and Mrs Gardiner had been hired two years before to run the Prep School and Niger House.

The first students in my dorm arrived on the Sunday afternoon, with their parents. I can't remember who they were but two of them had been boarders for a few years. Mr Gardiner asked them to look after me. It was comforting having other boys in my dorm who were going to guide me through the intricacies of that society.

I'd never eaten in a school dining room before. Mr Gardiner had shown it to me a few days before, and had explained that we in the Prep School had three tables to ourselves, about fifteen students per table with a prefect at the head of each table. And he pointed out that the long table in front of all the other tables was for the teachers and housemasters, who took turns controlling the dining room.

My first meal there was on Sunday evening, and because most of the boarders were yet to come, we used only a few of the tables, sitting anywhere we pleased. Many of the Niger students I was with, who'd been boarders before, complained about the food and only ate some of it. I didn't understand why. The food was in larger amounts, was more varied and was of better quality and taste than my normal fare at home. I was looking forward to three wholesome, healthy meals a day. And you could have as much milk as you liked – after all, Taranaki was one of the largest dairy provinces in New Zealand.

After dinner on Monday night we gathered in the sitting room for our first house meeting. By now I knew the other five boys in our dorm, as well as Lionel Brown, a Cook Islands student who'd arrived the day before. I sensed he was feeling just as homesick as I was, so felt a friendship growing quickly. We sat together in the crowded room.

The duty prefects quietened us down, and Mr Gardiner came in and stood in front of us. Smiling broadly he welcomed us, and then asked that we each rise and introduce ourselves. I avoided looking at him, in no way was I going first. He got the prefects to introduce themselves: name, where from and the number of years they'd been there. Instead of relaxing, my feelings of insecurity about my not being able to speak good English worsened. I relaxed a little when Lionel got through his introduction successfully. I got up and looking down at the floor, introduced myself in full sentences so as not to make mistakes.

One of the prefects handed out sheets of paper in which all the school and Niger House rules were printed. Mr Gardiner explained them quickly, then asked for questions – none. 'For the benefit of you new ones, you will address all your teachers as Sir, or Mister, or Miss or Mrs. You in turn will be addressed by your surname or Master. And you will at all times obey your teachers and prefects, and observe all the rules ... '

UNIFORMS
I didn't have school uniforms and other clothes I needed for school, so I had to wear my green suit, white shirt and tie to class. Two days later Mr Gardiner sent me with our Niger head prefect down to Hallensteins in the middle of the town with a long list of clothes I needed.

I'd never been in such a rich storehouse of clothes. I was astounded by its contents. The round bald-headed man who served us said, 'So we have another Island boy to outfit, eh?' He looked at our list. 'Yes, just like the others. Right.'

Within minutes he had measured me. And then he was methodically handing me clothes to try on. I didn't know where to undress and do that. 'Come this way, sir,' he said, leading me to a dressing room.

So for the next hour or so he handed me over the door the clothes to try on. I was acquiring more clothes than I'd ever had in my whole life. School uniforms, sweaters, shoes, school socks, dress socks, belts, underclothes, school blazer, long dress trousers, oilskin raincoat, towels, face cloths, etc. Such wealth, and it all smelled new and new and new. Often he got me to come out and stand in front of the full-length mirror where he ensured the clothes fitted properly.

When it was all done, I came out of the dressing room to find my clothes all wrapped and piled neatly on the counter. 'Don't worry about carrying them home,' he said. 'I'll ring Mr Gardiner and he'll come in his car and pick them up.'

That night Mr Gardiner got me to go into my dorm and unpack and put away my new clothes. Alone in the dorm, I lingered lovingly over the parcels, taking out my clothes, making sure they were folded properly, then, burying my face in some of them, inhaling their new, exhilarating smell. I had come into another world, a world of wealth, it felt. A world in which I didn't have to share my clothes with others, as I had to in Samoa. Clothes for every occasion and season.

That week Mrs Gardiner sewed name tags and my number into all my Hallenstein purchases. And she and Mr Gardiner showed me how to put on my full school uniform and cap, and how to wear them according to school regulations. 'Very handsome, Master Wendt,' she said. And for the first time, I started feeling at home in Palagi clothes.

And so I started fitting into that society. Only a few of us were totally new to the Prep School; most had already spent a few years there, some had enrolled when they'd been only in Standard One. John Perham, who became one of my closest friends, was one of those. His parents had split up and his aunt, who was his guardian, had put him into boarding school. Most of the boarders were sons of Waikato and Taranaki farmers, as there were few schools throughout those provinces then; their fathers were old boys of the school.

And if I thought I was homesick, a few others were more so. Two of them were still sobbing into the night, months after they arrived, and Mr Gardiner had to take them, like me, into their warm sitting room to sleep.

Looking back now, I think I fitted in well because the school and boarding house were similar to my own family and society: tightly knit, strict with clear rules and elders you had to obey, in a hierarchical structure in which you knew your place and role. The diet was plentiful and I no longer had to undergo periods of hunger. In terms of material things, I was better off than I'd ever been. I also felt safe and loved the learning and the sports, especially rugby, around which that school was built.

Apart from the Gardiners I also had other teachers who recognised my abilities and helped me develop them. Years later, I realised I'd developed effective protective mechanisms, strategies and attitudes to survive there. Throughout my time there, teachers and the principal described me in school reports as 'reticent, reserved, sometimes withdrawn, but is always pleasant, hard-working, and, when he is interested in something, he does outstanding work in it'. I loved the library (but hid that from my manly friends) and I also withdrew into books, becoming a bookworm, or so some of my friends said.

Like most institutions in New Zealand at the time, our boarding school was modelled on those of the 'mother country', England, and run by male teachers who'd survived the Second World War. Our principal was Colonel Gifford McNaught and most of our teachers had been military officers in the war. The school programme was geared towards fulfilling the philosophy of developing men who were tough, intelligent, resilient, loyal, brave and true comrades-in-arms who wouldn't wilt under pressure or pain. The warrior manliness of Sparta!

We had to wake at about 6.30 a.m., with the prefects in control, dress in our gym gear, jog round the town for about thirty minutes, return and survive cold showers (we enjoyed only one hot shower a week and even then for only three minutes each), make our beds to military perfection, dress in our school uniforms, line up and be inspected by the duty prefects for dress correctness, hurry to breakfast where we sat at tables in order of seniority, with the lowest sitting at the bottom of the table to collect all the dirty dishes, then return to our house, collect our books and anything else we needed for school, go to our classrooms, and then line up in the school assembly hall.

After school we trained or played the sports of the season, showered and dressed, and then had dinner, prep, lights out, sleep.

The first week of every school year was taken up with full-time military training, during which we all wore army uniforms and Colonel McNaught and his staff, decked in their military finery, trained us as if we were real army recruits. I was eventually made a sergeant. Soldiers, guns, marching, pretend war – a very enjoyable game!

WINTER ON ANIMAL FARM

But my first winter was a mainly miserable one. It was my first winter ever and for a long time I simply couldn't get used to the cold. It settled into my bones and didn't want to leave.

Mr Gardiner must have sensed that many of us were not settling easily into the cold months. He and Mrs Gardiner kept asking me if I was warm enough and though I lied that I was, they knew. At that time he also prescribed *Animal Farm* by George Orwell as one of our Form Two texts.

One Sunday evening, with the fire blazing in our sitting room, Mr Gardiner came in unexpectedly and told us he wanted to read *Animal Farm* to us. That will save those of you who don't like reading having to read it, he said. Some gave groans and moans but not too loudly.

We gathered in front of the fireplace in a semi-circle, with Mr Gardiner in an armchair, and many of us sitting or lying on the carpeted floor and on cushions.

He opened the novel and without any preliminary remarks, he read out the title, *Animal Farm* by George Orwell. And I immediately began to feel I was back in Samoa in my grandmother's fale, gathered around her listening to her fagogo. Then he began to read.

And for the whole of that winter, every Sunday night sang to Mr Gardiner's mesmerising voice as he unfolded the spellbinding satirical and allegorical tale of pigs and other animals and people competing for power and what that does to them. The rise and establishment of the totalitarian state, the loss of individual freedom and rights, the struggle to restore justice, equality and freedom of expression – they were themes that I would later find myself exploring in my writing. I have never forgotten that winter and how we loved both that tale and its teller – and how we came to our first understanding of power and how it corrupts us.

At the end of that year, 1953, I was dux of the Prep School. Much of that achievement I owed to Mr Gardiner's teaching and care and attention, though he never showed any obvious favouritism towards me. Being away from home and parents, I worked hard to live up to their expectations, and to distract myself from missing them and my brothers and sisters. And for me, learning in that new, stimulating environment, with the best facilities, equipment and materials, was a joy.

At the school prize-giving, I was awarded the dux's certificate and a leather-bound copy of *Kidnapped* by Robert Louis Stevenson. I think I still have that book buried somewhere in my mountain of papers and books.

7. MY MOTHER

My mother, Luisa, was born in 1915 and must have been about twenty-two or so when she married my father. She was the daughter of Patu Togi and Amy Fruean of Vaiala. He was one of the leading ali'i there. My mother's oldest brother was Tunupopo and her only sister was Fiapa'ipa'i; they had an adopted brother, Siliva.

Because her mother was part-European and fair with long almost-blonde hair and Palagi features, my mother had that colouring and hair and features too. (My Patu family always talked proudly of her having those Palagi features.)

There were no high schools at the time, so she had only a village primary school education, and, before she married my father, she spent her time serving her parents and aiga in Vaiala.

People who knew her always commented on

her beauty and the power of her soprano voice. Once when my student daughter Sina and I were enjoying a celebration of Samoan independence at Samoa House in Auckland, one of the elders of the Pacific Islanders' Congregational Church in Edinburgh Street, which my family attended, came up to us. Scrutinising Sina's face closely, Le Laulu Nonu asked: 'Are you Albert Wendt's daughter?' She nodded. 'You look just like your Dad's mother,' he said. Then turning to me, he said, 'Luisa was the most beautiful girl in Vaiala and we were all after her but she chose your ugly father!'

While I was at school in New Zealand, we had to write a letter to our parents every Friday night before we did our homework. The on-duty prefect would collect them at prep time and hand them to Mr Gardiner for posting. At least once a month, in response to my weekly letters, I would get a letter from my father, usually two pages long.

In March or April of 1954 I received a letter saying that my mother was ill, and my father was bringing her to Auckland Hospital. I concluded that she must be very ill. I don't think I told anyone at school. But I arranged with Mr Gardiner to spend my next school holidays in Auckland, with Ida and the NeeNees and with my father, who would be staying with them while my mother was in hospital.

Ida and my father were waiting for me at the Auckland railway station in the early morning. It was the first time my father had travelled out of Samoa, so I knew that his fears for my mother would be bundled up with apprehension about being in a foreign country. He was thinner and greyer, but still the tall, square-shouldered, muscular figure I'd always admired. I avoided looking up into his gaze, and when I did, I saw tears there before he embraced me.

'You're really grown up,' he said in Samoan, reaching down for my suitcase, but I grabbed it. Elders don't carry their children's things.

'Your mother is really looking forward to seeing you, Pati,' Ida said. 'She's been missing you all this time.'

'We'll go and see her this afternoon,' my father said, not looking at me.

The NeeNee children were unusually subdued, and treated me with enormous care as if I was already dressed in sorrow. Their parents had explained to them why my parents were in Auckland.

That afternoon, I dressed in my school uniform because Ida told me my mother would love to see me in it for the first time. She and my father and Aunt Moka praised the way I looked. 'And your mother's going to be really surprised by how much you've grown,' Aunt Moka said.

My father and I took a taxi to the hospital. Tightly I held the large bouquet of flowers Ida had bought for my mother. My heart beat at the back of my throat, and I tried to breathe quietly and not look at my father. He was gazing out through the taxi window, but I felt he was focused totally on how I might react to seeing my sick mother.

Six storeys up. A few others in the lift. We avoided looking at them.

I led my father out of the lift. He pointed to the right, and I followed him down the corridor.

The ward had two lines of beds against the walls under rows of windows. Most of the beds were occupied, and there were visitors around them. My father started heading for the middle bed against the far wall. A nurse in full uniform was bent over the patient – my mother? – and talking to her.

In the glow of the bright sunlight falling down from the windows, I recognised my mother's hair. My heart stopped beating in my throat. She was covered with a red blanket and over her right leg curved a stand, which kept the blanket and sheet off her leg.

'It is pain, it is much pain,' I heard her saying to the nurse. My mother didn't know much English. I stopped. My father clutched my hand gently and urged me forward. The nurse glanced up and recognised my father.

'Mrs Wendt, your husband is here,' the nurse said to my mother, who raised her head immediately and gazed over at me.

Her whole face broke into a wondrous joy – and also sorrow. Raising her arms towards me, she wailed once, then twice, and exclaimed, 'Si a'u kama e! Si a'u kama e!' ('My beloved child! My beloved child!') When I saw her arms and face and how thin she'd become, I hesitated, afraid for her safety. My father took the bouquet of flowers from me. I moved into her embrace. She swallowed her wailing and cried softly into my shoulder.

Not long after that, she made me stand up so she could inspect my appearance. 'Pati, ese fo'i lou lapo'a ma lou umi!', she said. ('You've grown so big and tall!')

My father and I sat down in the chairs beside her bed. I sensed most people in the ward were watching us. They were not looking at us directly but were curious, in a sympathetic way. They probably knew that my mother was ill with cancer.

While she held and caressed my right hand, my mother detailed for me how my brothers and sisters were and what they were doing. The pain in her face and eyes was gone. She stopped unexpectedly and then, her whole face flushed with pride, said in Samoan, 'By the way, we're so proud of you being dux last year. We told everyone in Samoa about it!' I didn't know what to say. She reached over and, running her forefinger down the side of my face, said, 'You have to keep working hard.'

Then she asked me to tell her about what I'd been doing that year.

For almost a week my father and I visited my mother every day – and sometimes Ida and Aunt Moka came too. My mother wasn't getting any better. She was on morphine most of the time.

On our way home one afternoon, my father informed me that my mother had had the choice of having her leg amputated. That would have stopped the cancer from spreading, but she'd chosen not to have the operation.

The next week my father said that I should be having a holiday, and gave me money to take my cousins to the movies instead of coming to the hospital. I went to the hospital only twice that week and simply sat beside her while she slept or talked about our life in Samoa. Ida gave me money too, and I went with my cousins to the Auckland War Memorial Museum.

'We're going home next week,' my father told me when we were with my mother. She gazed up at me. No sadness, total acceptance.

'I, Pati, lea o le a ma koe o i Samoa and vaai ou uso ma kuafafige ma le kakou aiga,' she said. ('Yes, Pati, we are returning to Samoa to care for your brothers and sisters and our family.')

During the next few days I didn't want to go and see her.

GOING HOME

It was a cloudless, windless day, rich with sun, with the sky doming above us, as the taxi drove Ida, Aunt Moka and Uncle Ron and I down to Mission Bay and the Sunderland air base. We wore our silence stoically, and avoided looking at one another.

The ambulance with my parents in it was already parked on the wharf, not far from where the large Sunderland aircraft sat in the water. Crew and other staff were preparing the aircraft. Passengers and their families and friends stood in groups near it.

The back doors of the ambulance were open and, as we walked towards it, my father and the main doctor and nurse who were looking after my mother came out of the open door. The medical staff went off to the wharf's edge and lit cigarettes.

My father took Moka, Ron and Ida into the ambulance. I stood at the bottom of the steps, feeling alone, afraid, utterly unwilling to be there. All around me the bay circled and circled and circled, so I sat down on the bottom step and, cupping my hands round my face, tried to steady the nausea that was returning.

When the others came out, they each caressed my head or shoulders as they went past. I noticed that they'd been crying; Moka was still drying her eyes, and Ron refused to look at me. 'I think your mother wants to see you,' Ida whispered.

My father looked down at me, his face grey, his eyes red from weeping. I forced myself up and staggered up the three steps. My father steadied me by wrapping his arm around my shoulders.

'He's here,' my father said to my mother, who was lying on the bed wrapped in a light white blanket on the right side of the ambulance. Under her head were two pillows, so she could see me. She patted the stool beside her in the aisle. I sat down and broke into silent tears, which worsened when she held my hands.

'Pau lava o le figagalo o le Akua,' she said slowly. No emotion. ('It is God's will.') I refused to look at her. I refused to accept it was God's will. I refused. 'Pati, you do good at school and come home e fesoasoagi i ou uso ma kuafafige ma lou kama.' Her speech and movements were slow, and I remembered she was heavily sedated with morphine to help keep the pain at bay.

A couple of relatives arrived and entered to say goodbye to my mother, so my father and I left the ambulance.

We walked out to the wharf's edge and stood with the doctor and nurse, looking down at our reflections in the still water. To our right, the crowd was now starting to form into two lines in front of two official desks, ready to check in for the flight.

'Loko koa, Pati,' my father said. 'Ga ma omai aua ga maga'o lou kiga e fa'akofa ia ke oe.' ('Be brave,

Pati. We came because your mother wanted to say goodbye to you.')

The Sunderland cruised out from the wharf and, turning left, went into the middle of the bay and stopped, facing east. Then – as I held my breath in my throat over the world I was losing – it pushed forward, gathering speed and parting the water, sending waves across the bay. Then it rose, rose and rose, up, up towards the blinding morning sun, taking my mother home.

When I got back to school, I didn't tell anyone.

Two weeks or so later I got a letter from my father. I knew what was in it. I slipped away from my friends and, hidden behind the locker rooms, ripped it open and read.

She'd died on 29 May 1954. She was only thirty-nine years old.

Many years ago, my sister Luisa, who lives in New Haven, America, told me that an American friend who'd read my novels had asked: 'How come there are so many orphans in your brother's novels?' Lu's reply to that was: 'Probably because he's been an orphan since he was thirteen years old and went to boarding school in New Zealand; our mother died two years later.'

Up to then I'd never thought of it that way. Lu's analysis seemed startlingly accurate. It was a painful revelation. I reread some of my novels – and found that Lu's friend's observation was unerring.

Yes, my novels are peopled with orphans, and my mother appears in various guises.

I was born out of a terrible separation at the end of 1952 from my mother and family, country and culture. The sea voyage on that banana boat was a week of constant seasickness and sometimes a wish to jump overboard and stop the rocking and dipping and diving as we penetrated deeper and deeper into the cold that is New Zealand. And then boarding school, and then the ultimate pain and inexhaustible sorrow of my mother's death. The sea voyage and her death are still vividly with me.

In that precarious, fearful separation from my aiga and in my mother's tragic death are the origins of my lifelong paranoia, anxiety and fears about travelling and living out of a suitcase – the source too of my expectation that all things and relationships are impermanent and the worst will always happen. I've travelled all over the world, mainly at the invitation and funding of others, but, to be truthful, I've not enjoyed a lot of it; nearly always I feel unsafe, insecure and stressed out about getting lost or suffering accidents and so forth. For most of my adult life I used to suffer duodenal ulcers, which threatened to bleed whenever I travelled, particularly to and around foreign countries. Many of my students and friends have throughout the years expressed envy at the amount of travelling I do, and they're surprised when I tell them I don't really enjoy it.

Like that of other people's, my life is founded on certain contradictions. I don't really like travelling – yet I do a lot of it. Is it that I unconsciously welcome stress and anxiety and punishing myself? That without that I'm not fully alive? Ulcers bleed out of such basic contradictions – and mine did until I met Reina.

8. THE WRITING

It was at New Plymouth that I got interested in writing, encouraged by teachers like Alan Gardiner, Terry Sweeney, whose textbook *Plain Sailing* was being used in all English courses in New Zealand high schools, Wit Alexander, who walked round the classroom quoting T. S. Eliot and W. B. Yeats, and Dick Braunton, who made New Zealand history come alive for me.

I published poems for the first time in the school magazine.

At Ardmore Teachers' College, from 1958 to 1959, I wrote and published more: essays, poems, stories. I wanted to explore all the genres – and that has continued to this day.

Then at Victoria University I published my first poems and stories in journals such as *Landfall*, *Mate*, *Thursday* and the *Listener*. And

I started writing my first novel, a very ambitious one – modelled on William Faulkner's intricate, sometimes convoluted, massive novels – which would be published years later as *Leaves of the Banyan Tree*.

I got married and returned with my wife Jenny to Samoa and taught at Samoa College. *Leaves of the Banyan Tree* was already a long manuscript and I couldn't see it being completed soon, so I left that and compiled a collection of poems titled *Inside Us the Dead*, and a collection of stories, *Flying-Fox in a Freedom Tree*. I was also finishing a short novel, *Sons for the Return Home*.

In 1970 Hone Tuwhare came and worked as a welder in the Canadian timber mill that was being built in Asau on the island of Savai'i. I admired his poetry greatly but hadn't met him. A friend, Tufuga Tupuola Efi, was Minister of Public Works, and he also loved Hone's work. Tufuga invited me to accompany him and other MPs and staff on a tour of government works round Savai'i.

Our convoy of cars arrived at the timber mill at mid-morning. The Canadian manager and his staff greeted us in a large tent they'd erected for the welcome. Tufuga immediately asked if we could meet the 'famous Māori poet Hone Tuwhare' who was working for them. The manager turned uncertainly to his staff. 'He's a welder and from New Zealand,' Tufuga added. One of the Samoan staff smiled, whispered to the manager, who nodded, and the Samoan staff member hurried off.

An embarrassed silence descended. Tufuga broke it by saying, 'Big operation you have here.' Immediately the manager started describing that operation and how the mill's construction was almost complete.

Hone was ushered in by the Samoan staff member who'd gone to fetch him. He was still dressed in the grease-stained overalls and cap he'd been using in his work. He recognised me and, bowing repeatedly, shuffled over and we hongied. I introduced him to Tufuga who shook his hand, and then they hongied.

During our hefty, delicious, scrumptious morning tea, our party and the Samoan staff members monopolised Hone, and the Canadians were left to help the waiting staff serve us.

Before Hone returned to New Zealand, he came and spent a weekend with my family in Apia.

Chuckling mischievously, he told us that our visit to the mill had changed his life there. After our party had left, the Canadians had treated him with unlimited generosity. He even got better accommodation and was asked to take his meals with the senior staff, but he rejected that because he would be isolated from his Samoan 'workmates'. The people of Asau and Vaisala villages near the mill also treated him like a high-ranking matai.

He asked me if I was working on anything. I told him I had three manuscripts.

When he got back to Auckland, he talked to Phoebe Meikle of Longman Paul about my manuscripts, and she wrote to me asking if she could look at them. I sent them to her.

She wanted to publish *Sons for the Return Home* – although she insisted there might not be a readership for Pacific writing. I said yes on the condition that she publish the other two books soon after. Collections of poetry and stories didn't sell many copies, she insisted. I insisted. And she agreed.

In 1973 *Sons for the Return Home* was published.

Then later *Inside Us the Dead*.

Then later *Flying-Fox in a Freedom Tree*.

The rest, as they say, is history.

I've always been grateful to Hone and Phoebe for that. She was also the best editor I've ever worked with.

ALUMNI MERITA

In early 2013 I received an email from Michael McMenamin, the headmaster of New Plymouth Boys' High, asking me if I would accept our Alumni Association's highest award, the Alumni Merita. Over the years I hadn't been a loyal and generous old boy nor a member of the Alumni Association, so I was surprised but I didn't hesitate in accepting the offer. Of the many awards I've received over the years, I consider this one the closest to my heart, closest to that homesick boy making friends with the Gardiners and becoming part of that school and Taranaki and my adopted country.

So about sixty years after I was in Prep School and Niger House, Reina drove us to New Plymouth. As soon as we entered Taranaki province, the Mountain held us in its welcoming gaze – and would do so until we left.

Since leaving the school in 1957, I'd visited it periodically. On our way this time we also stopped at Reina's old school, St Mary's in Stratford, not far from New Plymouth. We'd worked out that she'd been at Stratford at the time I was in New Plymouth. She'd been there with Viopapa Annandale from our scholarship group.

In New Plymouth we checked into a comfortable hotel near Ngamotu Beach, opposite the Govett-Brewster Art Gallery with its Len Lye collection.

And on a fine Monday morning, 15 April 2013, we drove up to the school. Michael McMenamin took us on a tour of the school, now much larger and more prosperous than I'd remembered it. Niger House had been sold and turned into apartments.

We went into the spacious library and were introduced to a large group of Pasefika students and some of their parents, a Samoan pastor and members of the New Plymouth Pacific Islands community, and some ex-students who'd been in the school when I'd been there. I didn't recognise any of my former colleagues; over fifty years had passed, and we were now old men.

We enjoyed a delicious lunch of Pasefika food. Afterwards I thanked them and presented the library with an almost complete set of all my fiction and poetry books.

About 1 p.m., accompanied by the headmaster and other guests, we headed for the assembly hall.

The whole route was lined by students, who broke into an exhilarating, powerful, mana-ful school haka that lifted us with joy and pride. I felt as if I was walking a few centimetres above the road, held up by my history at that school and all the people I'd known there and the promise of a marvellous life it held for me. It was a life now nearly over, being honoured by young men who reminded me of myself at their age. That haka I'll never forget.

1.15 p.m. The hall was packed with many parents, old boys and students. The students sat in their classes. On the stage were the staff, as I'd always seen them in assemblies. While the headmaster awarded some prizes, we waited. Moving memories of my time in those assemblies paraded through my sight. It only felt like yesterday.

Then Mr McMenamin introduced Reina and me to the audience. The head boy presented Reina with a bouquet of flowers. And the headmaster presented me with the Alumni Merita. The applause held me and raised me to my feet and the podium.

Here is some of my speech:

When I asked Michael about what I should talk about and for how long, he said three minutes maximum and give some advice to the students. I've never been good at giving advice to my children and mokopuna or to the hundreds of students I've taught, but I'll try my best.

When I was a student here standing in the old assembly hall waiting for a special guest to speak, I used to wonder what the dude was going to say, and then listen to him – be impressed or not impressed, and then not long after leaving the assembly, forget what he had said. I'm not optimistic enough to fool myself that many of you will remember what I'm going to say. But I'm egotistical and foolish enough to hope that some of you will wake up on the morning of your seventy-third birthday and remember that a seventy-three-year-old, silver-haired man with a permanent suntan spoke at your school assembly – but you can't remember what he said, though you feel if you don't remember it you won't go to heaven! So to our handsome students, all I ask is that you remember what I'm going to say and you'll go to heaven!

… The five years I spent here were some of the happiest years of my life. I didn't know it then, but those years shaped me and the directions my life would take. I made many close friends, and enjoyed and learned much from the teaching of some very special teachers, such as Alan Gardiner, Terry Sweeney, Wit Alexander and Dick Braunton.

Mt Taranaki also became a profound friend and one of the main mountains in my life.

I was fortunate that early in my life I discovered some of the things I felt passionate about and wanted to pursue, such as writing and telling stories. It was here I first started writing and publishing poetry and fiction – and over sixty years later I'm still doing it! My advice to you is to try and discover early the things you feel passionate about and go after them.

… Our lives are made up of great joy and love and pain and suffering and change and at times we feel like giving it all up. But don't forget it is the only life we have – so bear it, try and survive it, and enjoy it because it is the only life you will have! Live it with integrity and honesty and to the best of your gifts. And don't forget you're an integral part of a holistic world where everything is interconnected and you're responsible for keeping that intelligent unity healthy and alive and safe for the benefit of everything that is part of it.

Therein ends my sermon. I hope I've filled my three minutes, intelligently.

I wish our students and staff and school a successful future – whatever way you choose to interpret that term. May Taranaki continue to protect and bless our school and all of us.

singer is talking sadly to his beloved, Fa'ailoa, who, while he was away, got impatient and foolishly chose someone else. The song is about unrequited love and bitter disappointment about a life that could've been if she'd waited for him.

Strange that our mother, with her lilting guitar, chose to sing that to us as a lullaby, to calm us, send us to sleep. We all know that our journeys are, at times, tragic and disappointing, but we also know that with art, skill and invention we can use that suffering to fashion melodies that enable us to live with the pain, and even transcend it.

This song came out in the 1920s, and is still sung whenever Samoans gather. Like all art that is loved, it has outlived its composer and his Fa'ailoa, and is now a beautiful strand of the mat that is the life of those who know the song or who fall under its spell when they hear it. Whenever I hear it, my mother is with me in all her grandeur, grace and beauty.

My Mother Dances

Through the shadows cast by the moon tonight
the memory of my mother dances
like the flame-red carp I watched
in the black waters of the lake
of the Golden Pavilion in Kyoto.
Such burning grace.

Though I am ill with my future
and want to confess it to her
I won't. Not tonight.
For my mother dances
in the Golden Pavilion
of my heart.

How she can dance.
Even the moon is spellbound
with her grace.

Shaman of Visions (1984)

We are about those who have come before us, and those who are with us, and those to come, in an unbroken gafa of promise and possibility and becoming.

EDITORIAL NOTE

This is a list of the selected works by Albert Wendt that have been quoted in this BWB Text. Permission to quote from these works is gratefully acknowledged.

Flying-Fox in a Freedom Tree, Longman Paul, Auckland, 1974

Shaman of Visions, Auckland University Press/ Oxford University Press, Auckland, 1984

Ola, University of Hawai'i Press, Honolulu, 1995 (first published by Penguin, Auckland, 1991)

Black Rainbow, University of Hawai'i Press, Honolulu, 1995 (first published by Penguin, Auckland, 1992)

The Mango's Kiss, Vintage, Auckland, 2003

The Songmaker's Chair, Huia, Wellington, 2004, and first performed by the Auckland Theatre Company in 2003

From Mānoa to a Ponsonby Garden, Auckland University Press, Auckland, 2012

ABOUT THE AUTHOR

Maualaivao Albert Wendt has for many years been regarded as the Pacific's leading writer and a major influence on Pacific literature. His novels include *Leaves of the Banyan Tree* (which won the fiction section of the New Zealand Book Awards in 1980), *Ola* (which won the Commonwealth Book Prize for Southeast Asia and the Pacific in 1991), *The Mango's Kiss* and *Sons for the Return Home*. He is also a widely published poet and short story writer. Albert Wendt recently retired as Professor of English at the University of Auckland.

ABOUT BWB TEXTS

BWB Texts are short books on big subjects: succinct narratives spanning history, memoir, contemporary issues, science and more from great New Zealand writers. All BWB Texts are available digitally, with selected works also in paperback. New Texts are published monthly – visit www.bwb.co.nz to see the latest releases.

BWB Texts include:

The Quiet War on Asylum
Tracey Barnett

Thorndon: Wellington and Home: My Katherine Mansfield Project
Kirsty Gunn

The Inequality Debate: An Introduction
Max Rashbrooke

New Myths and Old Politics: The Waitangi Tribunal and the Challenge of Tradition
Tipene O'Regan

Growing Apart: Regional Prosperity in New Zealand
Shamubeel Eaqub

Barefoot Years
Martin Edmond

The Piketty Phenomenon: New Zealand Perspectives
Various

The Child Poverty Debate: Myths, Misconceptions and Misunderstandings
Jonathan Boston & Simon Chapple

Ruth, Roger and Me: Debts and Legacies
Andrew Dean

On Coming Home
Paula Morris

Haerenga: Early Māori Journeys Across the Globe
Vincent O'Malley

Generation Rent: Rethinking New Zealand's Priorities
Shamubeel & Selena Eaqub

No Country for Old Maids? Talking About the 'Man Drought'
Hannah August

Time of Useful Consciousness: Acting Urgently on Climate Change
Ralph Chapman